I RUSS ALAN PRINCE

I HANNAH SHAW GROVE

wealth management

I THE NEW BUSINESS
MODEL FOR FINANCIAL
ADVISORS

REVISED EDITION

WEALTH MANAGEMENT

❚ THE NEW BUSINESS MODEL FOR FINANCIAL ADVISORS

❚ BY RUSS ALAN PRINCE & HANNAH SHAW GROVE

WEALTH MANAGEMENT PRESS

9800 Metcalf Avenue
Overland Park, KS 66212

ISBN number 0-9726652-1-8

To Jerry and his best friend Ace, the two silliest.
— RUSS

For access and possibilities, to Nidbo.
— HANNAH

table of contents

foreword
to The revised edition

What do affluent Americans want from their financial advisors?

Those of us in the financial services industry know just how hard it is to answer this crucial question. As Americans have become wealthier – and there are more millionaires today than ever before – there are also more firms vying for their attention, their trust, and their assets. That's why the above question is so pertinent. By better understanding what the affluent want, we'll be better able to get their attention, win their trust, and – if we do our job right – take the lead in managing their financial affairs.

Based on my practical experience, the answer to this question is straightforward: the affluent want it all. More precisely, they want to centralize and simplify their financial lives in the hands of one trusted advisor who knows them and can bring in other experts to address any issue that may come up, from buying bonds to writing a will, from hedging concentrated stock to exploring offshore asset protection. That comprehensive and consultative approach is the essence of successful wealth management – and it's what this book is all about.

The wealth management model outlined in this book, which first came out in 2003, is valuable for one compelling reason: it works. The authors not only make a persuasive case for why we should adopt wealth management, but they show us how to do so in a practical, step-by-step way.

Hannah Shaw Grove and Russ Alan Prince are ideally positioned to provide that direction. They have teamed up on some of the most far-ranging research studies of the affluent and their advisors over the past decade, and they also have extensive first-hand experience in putting what they've learned to work with high-net-worth clients and leading financial advisors. For those of us looking to give affluent clients what they want, there could be no better guides – and handbook – as we aspire to be collaborative with one another, consultative with our clients, and comprehensive in our offerings.

DAVID S. BAGATELLE
EXECUTIVE VICE PRESIDENT, SIGNATURE BANK
PRESIDENT & CEO, SIGNATURE SECURITIES
MARCH 2005

List of exhibits

CHAPTER 8: ESTABLISHING NEW CLIENT RELATIONSHIPS

introduction
The promise of wealth management

During the last decade, the stock market enjoyed an unprecedented bull run that led many investors to believe annual returns of 20% or better were pretty much a sure thing. Throw a dart. Pick a mutual fund. Reap the rewards.

In that same ten-year period, the stock market suffered through its longest and most painful downturn since the end of the Depression. Few sectors, styles – or portfolios – emerged unscathed, and chastened investors sought refuge in bonds and money market funds despite the record-low yields.

Throughout the decade, the stock market also set new standards for volatility and unpredictability that left many affluent investors looking for financial guidance. The elixir often prescribed – wealth management – may indeed be the best remedy for what ails those investors, but it's also often imperfectly understood and improperly administered.

ı what ıs wealth management?

Wealth management, simply defined, is the ability of an advisor or advisory team to deliver a full range of financial services and products to a client in a consultative way. That means, for example, offering a client brokerage services as well as insurance, estate planning, and guidance when it comes to charitable giving. Importantly, that broader relationship is not inextricably linked to the ups and downs of the stock market because there are objectives and components other than the Dow and the NASDAQ to factor in. That tends to insulate wealth managers from being judged solely on the basis of their investment performance. Moreover, because the relationship is many faceted – it's about far more than investments alone – a stronger bond is created between the client and his or her wealth manager.

Equally important, a wealth manager must connect with each client on a highly personal level so the client can see how the range of financial solutions being offered is specifically designed to meet his or her needs by an understanding and insightful professional. In the context of wealth management, peace of mind achieved through the solving of financial problems is as important as profit; for some affluent clients, more so.

I A New Generation of Affluent Investors

One of the driving premises behind the growth of wealth management is the fact that affluent investors have higher expectations of their financial advisors than they did a decade or even just a few years ago. Compared with investors of an earlier era, today's wealthy clients are usually more informed about investing, often far more involved in their financial affairs, and generally more demanding, if for no other reason than that they think they can do it themselves (or, at least, do no worse than their financial advisors), an option that would have never dawned on their parents. The passive high-net-worth investor who hands over his or her assets to an advisor and stands clear is all but extinct.

For those financial advisors who successfully make the move to wealth management, there are, as we shall see, substantial rewards: a better working relationship with individual clients, greater profitability per client, and more referrals. But making the transition is not as simple as printing new business cards that read "Wealth Manager." Along the way, you'll have to address such thorny issues as which clients to keep and how to transition the others. You'll have to know which wealth management services to deliver yourself and how to access the rest. You'll also have to find the right specialists to partner with. And you'll most probably have to get used to a higher and more consultative standard of client contact. That's a lot to think about – and a lot to do.

┃ what the surveys say

To understand the mechanics of wealth management, we have conducted some 40 surveys of affluent investors and their advisors during this crucial and transitional decade that have involved upwards of 18,000 respondents. We have asked clients about their preferences, their behavior, and their relationships with their advisors. And we have asked advisors about their challenges, business models, and relationships with their clients. In study after study, affluent investors have told us that they want a primary source of solutions for their financial life – the wealth management model – and that they believe in advisory relation-ships; they're not looking to go it alone. But we've also found that such integrated financial solutions are seldom being delivered. In fact, there's often a startling disconnect between what wealthy clients want and what their financial advisors are giving them.

This book was written to help you understand the challenges of wealth management, as well as what those challenges mean for the way you do business. Based on our extensive research and our knowledge of industry best practices, we've identified what we believe to be the optimal wealth management platform and also separately designed and developed the curriculum and training to help advisors adopt it. For this book, we have created a series of self-assessment tools to help you decide whether or not you're well-suited to become a wealth manager; to enable you to better "think" like a wealth manager; to help you evaluate your ability to access the necessary resources so that you can offer a range of financial services and products; and to better understand how to persuade your clients, prospects, and potential sources of referrals that you've successfully made the transition to the wealth management model.

As noted, the move to wealth management is not an easy one — and it may not be right for you. Yet it's one that every financial advisor should consider because of the great profit potential of such a model and because, increasingly, affluent clients prefer to partner with wealth managers, not financial advisors.

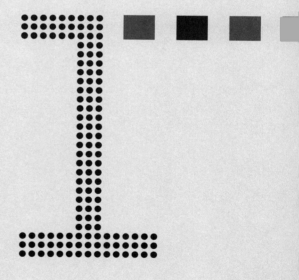

**| THE CASE FOR
WEALTH MANAGEMENT**

wealth management defined

wealth management is a popular concept and pitch, but one that is nonetheless variously defined. Those in the financial services industry might have a slightly different spin on it than those in the accounting or insurance field. For the purpose of this book, however, we define wealth management as:

> ▎ Delivering a full range of interrelated brokerage, investment, and advanced planning services and products to affluent clients in a highly consultative way.

▏ The Division of Financial Labor

Traditionally, the affluent have relied on one provider for each financial product and service. The broker took care of the portfolio, the insurance agent the life insurance, the lawyer trusts and estate planning, and the accountant taxes. The various providers might interact occasionally, but by-and-large their services were compartmentalized – and that was the service model that clients preferred (or at least thought they did).

Recently, however, there's been a proliferation of services and products targeting the affluent. There's also been a gradual evolution in the advisory model toward one where the client and advisor engage in a more personal and professional relationship, where products and services are customized to suit each affluent client's specific needs and goals. Wealth management is the result of these trends. (These trends will be examined in greater detail in the next chapter.)

There's a simple premise at work here: As being wealthy becomes more and more complicated, the affluent are increasingly inter-ested in centralizing and streamlining their financial lives, preferably through the retention of a lead advisor – the wealth manager. As the affluent address the challenges of being wealthy, they don't want to have to work with a different advisor for every product and service.

A 1998 study that we conducted among 778 investors with a net worth of at least $5 million underscored the desire of the affluent to consolidate services, as well as the potential benefits for the advisors involved. In fact, when it came to the number of services provided, the level of client satisfaction soared from 39.9% for those clients getting one service to an impressive 96.1% for those getting three or more services (Exhibit 1.1). The increase in the number of referrals relative to the number of services offered was similarly steep, with those advisors who provided three or more services being nearly three times as likely to have received two or more referrals from those clients in the preceding year (Exhibit 1.2). It's that desire to streamline their financial lives that makes wealth management so appealing to the affluent.

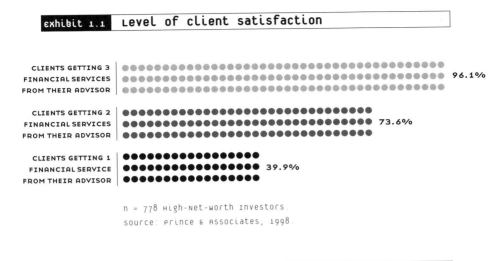

| exhibit 1.1 | Level of client satisfaction |

CLIENTS GETTING 3
FINANCIAL SERVICES   96.1%
FROM THEIR ADVISOR

CLIENTS GETTING 2
FINANCIAL SERVICES   73.6%
FROM THEIR ADVISOR

CLIENTS GETTING 1
FINANCIAL SERVICE   39.9%
FROM THEIR ADVISOR

n = 778 High-Net-Worth Investors.
Source: Prince & Associates, 1998.

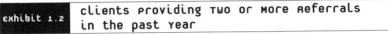

| exhibit 1.2 | Clients providing two or more referrals in the past year |

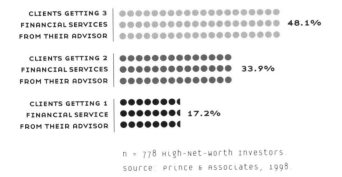

CLIENTS GETTING 3
FINANCIAL SERVICES   48.1%
FROM THEIR ADVISOR

CLIENTS GETTING 2
FINANCIAL SERVICES   33.9%
FROM THEIR ADVISOR

CLIENTS GETTING 1
FINANCIAL SERVICE   17.2%
FROM THEIR ADVISOR

n = 778 High-Net-Worth Investors.
Source: Prince & Associates, 1998.

Clearly, the more services and products you can offer a wealthy client, the stronger your relationship – and the better your business. And the consultative nature of wealth management lends itself to providing that range of interrelated services and products.

▎A Three-part equation

As noted, wealth management is a three-part equation: brokerage, investment management, and advanced planning. Brokerage encompasses the transaction side of the investment business, chiefly the buying and selling of stocks and bonds. Brokerage also includes transactions such as hedging concentrated stock positions. For the purposes of our discussion, the investment side entails asset management services such as managed accounts, mutual funds, fee-based brokerage accounts, and alternative investments including hedge funds, funds of funds, real estate, and private equity funds.

These first two components are not only the foundation of wealth management but also the ones that most participants in the financial advisory business are already familiar and comfortable with. That's less the case with advanced planning, which is in many ways the defining element of wealth management; that is, what makes wealth management both attractive to clients – especially wealthier ones – and viable to financial advisors.

▎Why Advanced planning?

There are four sets of services that are considered to be accretive to brokerage and investment management. They are:

▌ Advanced planning (covering wealth enhancement, wealth transfer, asset protection, and charitable giving);

▌ Credit (including mortgages as well as personal loans and, for business owners, commercial loans);

▌ Property and casualty insurance; and

▌ Administration and accounting services.

Given those four options, how did we determine that advanced planning would be best suited to the wealth management model, the skills of financial advisors, and the needs of affluent clients?

To determine which set (or sets) of services should be added to brokerage and investment management to build a wealth management platform, we conducted an analysis based on three key variables:

I Risk-adjusted returns;

I Ease of integration; and

I The relationship-enhancement opportunity.

We examined data from 815 successful brokers who had adopted the wealth management model as well as another 593 independent financial planners who had built multimillion-dollar wealth management practices. With regard to each of the above variables, a rating of 1.00 was defined as an optimal (if, in reality, unattainable) rating. Here's what we found.

Perhaps most persuasively, when it came to making the case for advanced planning, it offered the highest risk-adjusted returns (Exhibit 1.3), eclipsing even credit where there's always the risk of default or bankruptcy.

exhibit 1.3 **Risk-Adjusted Returns**

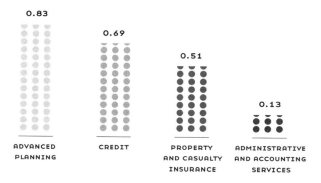

n = 815 Brokers & 593 Independent Financial Planners
Source: Prince & Associates, 2001

When considering ease of integration, however, advanced planning finished a distant fourth (Exhibit 1.4), and one can easily imagine the difference between getting a margin loan – a matter of a phone call – and putting together a comprehensive wealth management platform that might entail, for example, correcting a flawed split-dollar plan to provide the intended benefits without any adverse legal consequences. Wealth management is far from a snap. Of course, as Exhibit 1.3 shows, the added effort can lead to a greater profit margin.

 **exhibit 1.4** **ease of integration**

n = 815 Brokers & 593 Independent Financial Planners.
source: Prince & Associates, 2001.

Finally, as illustrated by Exhibit 1.5, the very consultative nature of advanced planning that can make it highly challenging and complicated also creates an opportunity to extend a relationship in ways that the other sets of services do not. The advanced planning process includes profiling clients and their coming to understand how they feel about such personal issues as their children (through an estate plan) and their charitable legacy (through philanthropic giving). The intimacy and problem-solving orientation adds up to a deeper client connection which can, in turn, result in a stronger relationship, greater profitability per client, and more referrals.

| exhibit 1.5 | relationship enhancement |

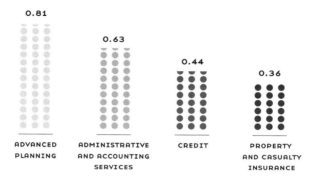

n = 815 brokers & 593 independent financial planners.
source: prince & associates, 2001.

Of course, a wealth manager does not adopt advanced planning to the exclusion of the other sets of services; every affluent client will need each of them at some point. But those other services are not necessarily integral to the shape and profitability of the wealth management model. They are, therefore, subsidiary to the core model, subsets of wealth management, but ones that can further burnish a wealth manager's credentials by allowing him or her to summon and guide other top advisors to the affluent. Credit, property and casualty insurance, and administrative and accounting services can – and most probably will – be part of the wealth management platform, but they do not present the same opportunity for interacting with the affluent.

ı A closer Look at Advanced Planning

Having empirically established that advanced planning is an essential part of the wealth management model because it results in the maximum revenue and a deeper understanding of the affluent client, it's time to take a closer look at precisely what it entails.

As noted, advanced planning comprises the following four inter-woven components: wealth enhancement, wealth transfer, asset protection, and charitable giving. Keep in mind that you wouldn't have to be able to personally deliver each of these components; you would, however, have to be able to demonstrate a broad understanding of each, an idea of how and where they fit into the wealth management model, and also have access to a professional network that can handle the implementation. Here's more detail about each of the four components.

wealth enhancement: Tax management strategies to improve overall investment performance. No one likes to pay taxes, and advisors to the affluent are particularly innovative when it comes to finding ways to legally lessen the tax bite on investment proceeds. The ideal scenario would be to move from short-term capital gains to long-term capital gains to deferred taxes to no taxes. The key is for clients, guided by their wealth managers, to determine the current timing, nature, and amount of taxable income – to manage which taxes are paid and when. To minimize taxes, wealth managers rely on such tools as contingent swaps, prepaid forwards, charitable remainder trusts, and cashless collars.

wealth transfer: Personalized and tax-efficient estate planning. As long as there are estate taxes, as long as there are intergenerational considerations, and as long as there are inter-connected business interests, there will be a demand for tax-efficient wealth transfer strategies and tactics. Basic estate planning employs such strategies as credit-shelter trusts and life insurance. For those clients with a more complicated financial picture and goals, there are more sophisticated wealth-transfer strategies such as self-canceling installment notes and remainder purchase marital trusts.

Asset Protection: **Risk management strategies to protect assets from litigants, creditors, and family members.** This is a subset of risk management with the aim of shielding the client's wealth from creditors, litigants, children, in-laws, and ex-spouses. The strategies include liability insurance, disassociation, and transformation. As often as not, the most effective strategy is a function of the sophistication and tactics of the opposition.

Charitable Giving: **Meeting personal philanthropic inclinations with opportunities for wealth enhancement and transfer.** Giving is an integral part of the American way of life and the country's annual contributions have recently passed the $200 billion mark. Clearly, the affluent want to give something back. Many of the wealthy also want to enjoy the prestige and visibility that goes with charitable giving, whether it's a matter of seeing their name in the newspapers or on a building. Strategies for making charitable donations include private foundations, donor-advised funds, charitable remainder trusts, and charitable lead trusts.

connecting with clients

To reiterate, advanced planning is an essential part of the wealth management framework not only because of the services it comprises, but because of the way in which the advanced planning process develops. Writing wills, protecting wealth from litigants, donating money, and passing the control of businesses are all life decisions that involve a lot of one-to-one time. Those meetings create an environment of connection and consultation that has been shown to be the precursor of a more profitable relationship. At this high level, clients want to be communicated with and understood, not sold to.

⏐ The opportunity

Of course, not every advisor can deliver on every aspect of wealth management: brokerage, investment, and advanced planning. But that should not be an impediment; it's precisely the point and the opportunity. Through your firm and/or through an independent but highly qualified professional network, you can arrange for all of these services and be the conduit through which they pass to the client. You'll continue to concentrate on your given specialty, whether it's brokerage, investing, advanced planning, or some subset of the three, but you'll now be able to identify a much wider array of client needs and desires and be able to bring the requisite expertise to the table. In addition, you'll be in a position to manage a broader and more profitable relationship with each affluent client. Finally, there will be more assets to manage per client and more referrals from the affluent client. These are opportunities that don't exist to the same degree in a traditional financial advisory relationship.

⏐ The profit potential

Research has shown that the affluent like the idea of wealth management. For the advisor, there is another compelling argument in favor of the wealth management model that has already been alluded to: increased profitability.

Wealth management is a way of working with clients, but it's also a platform for a wide range of products and services. Furthermore, it offers you the opportunity to cross-sell a number of different but interrelated services and products to one client. And wealth

management is different from traditional brokerage and investment management because it combines four compensation
arrangements that can add up to greater profitability. They are:

  I **Advisory fees**: Sometimes hourly-based but more
    often project-based, advisory fees range from several
    thousand dollars to six figures, and they're most
    commonly charged for planning and feasibility studies
    as well as case design and implementation.

  I **Commissions**: Advisors can receive commissions on the
    sale of securities, certain classes of mutual funds,
    derivatives transactions, and life insurance.

  I **Asset-based fees**: The most pervasive form of asset-
    based fee is for fee-based money management as in
    the case of a managed account or investment consulting
    where the wealth manager constructs and monitors
    the client's portfolio.

  I **Performance fees**: Potentially the most profitable form
    of compensation, a performance fee is either based on
    the success of a specific wealth management strategy
    (or strategies) or tied to certain products such as
    hedge funds.

While it's not necessary to use all or even more than one of the
above compensation models to increase revenue, the opportunity
to do so certainly exists. In fact, the majority of wealth managers
tend to employ the same compensation structures that they used as
financial advisors. Over time, on a case-by-case basis that hinges
on the nature of a given client relationship, they might adopt a
new compensation model and slowly integrate it into their
business, but that's not always the case. We have, however,
worked with many financial advisors who more than doubled their
production in the course of just a few years by moving from a
commissions-only or commissions and asset-based compensation
model to a platform that included all four models. The final
decision is yours and it's based on what you believe will work best
for you and your clients.

⎪ Not Just New Clients

The use of the wealth management model is not restricted to new clients, of course; it can also lead to greater profitability from existing clients. In fact, many advisors who make the transition find that leveraging the already-strong relationships they have with their current clients, a more forgiving audience perhaps than those who don't know you, is the best way to jump-start their wealth management practices. It's also easier to arrange a meeting with an existing client, a phone call rather than a cold call is all that it takes, and you know enough about them to build a compelling case for wealth management. That makes for both greater rapport and a shorter sales cycle.

Also, as we shall see in Chapter 3, wealth management can insulate both investors and their advisors during economic downturns because it's less directly linked to the stock market. With the broader relationship that's at the heart of wealth management and with non-correlated investments such as hedge funds, there are other ways for your performance to be measured, including, for example, whether or not you're proactive about staying in contact with your clients.

⎪ The Wealth Manager Checklist

We've defined wealth management and shown why it's attractive to both high-net-worth investors and their advisors. Now it's time to take a brief look at what it takes to be a wealth manager – and whether or not it's right for you.

In the course of this book, we'll discuss in greater detail the hows and whys of wealth management: connecting with clients; building and managing a professional network; keeping up with the latest trends, products, and services; thinking like a wealth manager; and positioning oneself as a wealth manager with clients, prospects, and fellow advisors. In the meantime, here are the key attributes of a wealth manager, based upon our research among affluent clients and financial advisors who've successfully made the transition to the wealth management model:

1. Establish and maintain a high-touch, consultative relationship with each affluent client;

2. Serve as the affluent client's general contractor or personal CFO for the full slate of wealth management products and services (brokerage, investment management, and advanced planning);

3. Assemble and manage a team of specialists that can deliver those products and services that are outside of your personal area of expertise; and

4. Be familiar enough with each client's situation to know when to bring in specialists.

That's a lot to do and, for some financial advisors, a giant leap. But we believe that now is the time to weigh whether a move to the wealth management model makes sense for you and for your business.

case study

The Art of Wealth Management

Marie has a highly-appreciated old master that's been in her family for generations, but she's currently short on cash. She could make a lot of money by selling the painting at auction, but she'd also have to pay punishing capital gains. By adopting a wealth management approach, however, she could sell the painting through a charitable remainder trust. That way she would avoid the taxes and the hard asset could be transformed into liquid assets that, as her wealth manager, you could invest and potentially profit from.

self-diagnostic

ⓘ assessing your potential

using the following scale, rate how satisfied you are with each of the following business objectives:

not at all satisfied   *extremely satisfied*

| < | 1 | 2 | 3 | 4 | 5 | 6 | 7 | 8 | 9 | 10 | > |

ⓘ YOUR CURRENT INCOME ☐

ⓘ YOUR FUTURE IN THE FINANCIAL SERVICES BUSINESS ☐

ⓘ YOUR ABILITY TO GET WEALTHIER CLIENTS ☐

ⓘ YOUR OVERALL PRODUCTION ☐

ⓘ YOUR CAPACITY TO LEVERAGE YOUR EXISTING
  CLIENT RELATIONSHIPS INTO MORE BUSINESS ☐

ⓘ YOUR ABILITY TO AVOID LOSING IMPORTANT CLIENTS ☐

ⓘ YOUR CAPACITY TO GENERATE SIGNIFICANT ASSET GROWTH
  IRRESPECTIVE OF THE PERFORMANCE OF THE MARKETS ☐

                                          TOTAL ☐

Now add up your score. If you have a score of **35** or less, then you should consider the wealth management model (a successful wealth manager would get a score of 56 or more on this self-diagnostic).

Finally, consider how wealth management is a solution to each of these issues:

ISSUE	THE WEALTH MANAGEMENT SOLUTION
YOUR CURRENT INCOME	By creating a broad, consultative relationship, wealth management sets the stage for you to provide additional revenue-generating products and services, gather more assets, and get more referrals from both existing clients and centers of influence — the attorneys and accountants who work with the wealthy.
YOUR FUTURE IN THE FINANCIAL SERVICES BUSINESS	Our extensive research has established that most affluent clients are highly receptive to the wealth management model and that it also enhances your ability to differentiate yourself from other advisors.
YOUR ABILITY TO GET WEALTHIER CLIENTS	Based on the psychology and preferences of the affluent, the wealth management model is one of the best ways to attract and retain them as clients.
YOUR OVERALL PRODUCTION	Because of your deeper understanding of your affluent clients, you'll have more touchpoints to capitalize on and more products and services to offer.
YOUR CAPACITY TO LEVERAGE YOUR EXISTING CLIENT RELATIONSHIPS INTO MORE BUSINESS	Since you have a strong working relationship with, and an informed perspective of, your current clients, they'll be receptive to the wealth management model and what it can do for them, further solidifying the relationship while potentially increasing your profitability.
YOUR ABILITY TO AVOID LOSING IMPORTANT CLIENTS	With the consultative nature of wealth management and the broader menu of products and services that you'll be able to offer in an integrated way, you'll forge strong interpersonal bonds that can help you withstand periods of poor investment performance.
YOUR CAPACITY TO GENERATE SIGNIFICANT ASSET GROWTH IRRESPEC- TIVE OF THE PERFORMANCE OF THE STOCK MARKET	Many of the services and products of wealth manage- ment, such as life insurance, are not tied to the stock market or even to investing.

CHAPTER 2

The Trends Behind the Wealth

I A RECORD NUMBER OF AMERICAN MILLIONAIRES

I THE RISE OF THE STOCK MARKET

I AN INCREASINGLY COMPLICATED FINANCIAL PROFILE
FOR WEALTHY INVESTORS

I GREATER INVOLVEMENT OF THE AFFLUENT IN THEIR
FINANCIAL AFFAIRS

I MORE AVAILABLE FINANCIAL INFORMATION THAN
EVER BEFORE

I AN EXPRESSED DESIRE ON THE PART OF THE AFFLUENT
FOR A CONSULTATIVE RELATIONSHIP

I MORE ADVISORS PER AFFLUENT CLIENT

When and why did the traditional advisory model – a given financial advisor for each financial service and product – fall from favor? Since when has "just" being a broker or a financial consultant not been enough?

∎ The Rise of the American Millionaire

The passage from financial advisor to wealth manager begins with the growing number of American millionaires. Here in the United States, the ranks of the rich have always been open to all comers; the self-made millionaire is as important a national icon as the bald eagle or Uncle Sam. But never before have those ranks swelled as they did during the 1990's. No one seems to agree on the number of millionaires in America today – the estimates range from two million to eight million – but there is a general consensus that there have never been more millionaires than there are right now. And whichever end of the estimate one favors, there's no denying that the rate of increase has been staggering; in 1975, by comparison, there were estimated to be just 90,000 millionaires in the United States.

There are a lot of reasons for the rise in affluence, but reason number one is indisputable: the stock market. In 1980, the Dow opened at 839. In 2000, it opened at 11,497. It has since been battered by a recession and a raft of corporate accounting scandals but, as we went to press, the Dow had still increased by tenfold in the last two decades, an unprecedented run-up.

At the same time (and very much because of the steady surge), Americans have never had more money invested in the stock market as measured by both dollars and numbers. A generation ago, the stock market was seen by many as a casino where only the very wealthy dared dabble. Today, with the rise of the 401(k) and the mutual fund, everyone seems to have a stake in the game. Mutual funds surpassed banks as the major repository of American savings sometime in the late 1990's. According to the Investment Company Institute, nearly half of all American households – 54.2 million – owned mutual funds at the start of 2003, and the number of individuals owning funds was 95 million. The total net assets of mutual funds increased from $1.6 trillion at year-end 1992 to $6.4 trillion at the end of 2002.

Everyone was not fortunate enough to have ridden the bull market from start to finish, of course, and many late-comers were battered by the collapse of the dot.coms and the subsequent recession. But the fact remains that anyone who's stayed in the stock market for the last decade is almost certainly still well ahead of the game.

As an aside, it could be argued that the long success of the stock market in some ways stunted the broad development of a more holistic client/advisor relationship. As long as the boom continued, it was hard for a financial advisor to go wrong, investment-wise. Encouraged by online trading, many investors also took to going it alone. Neither trend was good for the long-term health of the advisory business, and when the bull market ended the weakness of the model was quickly exposed. Many advisors were suddenly being judged by a single yardstick, returns, and falling short. Investors who had been do-it-yourselfers quickly retreated and looked to their advisors for help as the value of their portfolios shrank. Relationships had to be reconsidered and rebuilt. And it is in just such an environment that wealth management, not tied to the fortunes of the stock market, could flourish at last.

ı with wealth comes complexity

As a result of their wealth, the new affluent have an increasingly complicated financial profile – and far more financial options to consider. To a certain extent, the opportunity for high-end financial advisors that has been created is simply a matter of scale; since there are that many more millionaires, there are that many more people who have to address challenging investment, tax, legal, insurance, and inheritance issues. But there are also more products to choose from; exchange-traded funds, 529s, donor-advised funds, and managed accounts to name but a few. This complexity is too overwhelming for most individuals to take on, especially for those who are new to wealth, and our research has shown that they have no disposition to do so. Even the majority of those who have been wealthy for some time are aware of an increasingly challenging financial world. From the flow of infor- mation to the vast array of available products and services to the ever-changing tax and regulatory environments, the issues, tools, and rules affecting the wealthy have never been as hard to keep up with.

Further, the wealthy do not as a rule want to merely park their money in a savings account at a bank. They're aiming higher. They generally want to diversify across a wide range of styles and vehicles, to concentrate on wealth enhancement strategies and tactics that maximize tax efficiency. Almost all affluent clients want to make sure they can maintain their lifestyle at the same time that they appropriately provide for the next generation. Financial services firms, accountants, and attorneys have been diligent in developing products, services, and strategies that will help the affluent achieve these goals.

Yet our studies of the affluent show that their interest in financial products and services designed for people in their wealth bracket far exceeds their use of such products and services. In other words, when they become wealthy they want access to the financial perks that have up until then been denied them, but they've not yet taken advantage of those perks, a trend demonstrated in the results of a study of 329 individuals with investable assets of at least $1 million that we conducted in 2001 (Exhibit 2.1).

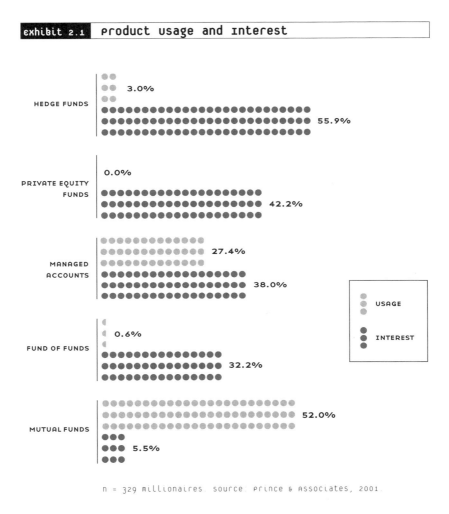

| exhibit 2.1 | product usage and interest |

n = 329 millionaires. source: prince & associates, 2001.

This research tells us that, in order to work with affluent investors, you need to not only understand the state-of-the-art products and advisory services, but also be able to access and deftly introduce them to your affluent clients. Your opportunity lies in the fact that, in many cases, financial advisors have not accurately assessed and proactively addressed the level of their clients' interest in such products and services.

❙ Today's Investors Are Involved and Informed

There are other factors at play in the rise of the wealth manager and the changing role of the traditional financial advisor. For starters, today's wealthy investors tend to be far more involved in their financial affairs. A number of America's affluent investors are first-generation millionaires and many are self-made and self-employed. As such, they're used to being involved in any major financial decision-making. They don't need to make every call, but they do need to understand their options and see why any decision makes sense for them from both the personal and financial standpoints.

To accommodate that level of interest and involvement in their own affairs, there's a staggering amount of financial information available for investors today that promotes and explains financial products and services, mostly via the Internet. Plug "investing" or "mutual funds" into a search engine and you'll get millions of citations and come-ons. Narrow the search to "hedge funds" and there will still be hundreds of thousands of citations to sift through. Investors can also check their portfolios or visit rating agencies at any time of the day or night. And many firms have touted the online availability of research reports that used to only be available to analysts or institutional investors.

The welter of information takes its toll, however. While affluent investors are informed, they're also overwhelmed. A number of studies conducted over the past few years have shown that the more closely investors follow their portfolios, and the more actively they trade, the less successful they are. Information leads to overconfidence, overconfidence leads to more trading, and more trading by individual investors all too often leads to poor performance. It's also particularly hard for individuals to adhere to buy and sell disciplines and to keep sight of their long-term objectives. Without perspective, all of the information in the world can still add up to chaos.

Further, stock market volatility has become a way of life in the last few years, with the major market indexes swinging up and down by a point or two more often during a single week than they used to in an entire month or year. In 2002, for instance, about one trading day in two saw the S&P 500 and the Dow rise or fall more than 1%, and on average they had moves of at least 2% once a week. For the S&P, the volatility was the highest since 1938; for the Dow, since 1933. That new volatility – hypervolatility – combined with a bear market, has discouraged investors from trading both on their own and online, and led many wealthy investors to value the guidance of their financial advisors more than ever before.

ı Looking for professional financial help

Take wealth, add a measure of financial complexity and information overload, stir in volatility and a recession, and it's hardly surprising that – for all of their independence and entrepreneurship – America's affluent still rely on professional financial advisors, valuing both their expertise and the research and analysis they can tap into on their clients' behalf.

Whether we've studied people who have inherited millions, made millions, or intend to donate millions, there is one constant: they want to work with a financial professional. They don't want to go it alone. And those same studies have shown that, their facility with the Internet notwithstanding, affluent investors don't want to work with an online advisor; they want a flesh-and-blood resource. To cite just one such study that we conducted in 2000, a full 98.2% of 611 investors with $500,000 or more in investable assets said they would rather go to an advisor than a website.

The affluent would also rather work with an advisor who caters to the wealthy (Exhibit 2.2). In another study we conducted in 2000 among 388 people who had inherited at least $1 million in the previous three-to-five years, better than four out of five of the inheritors wanted an investment advisor who specialized in working with wealthy clients, and a similar percentage expected those advisors to give them access to previously unavailable investments. Once they had money, they wanted the higher-end advisors and products to match their new financial status.

In a second study of 334 people who had inherited at least $1 million in the previous two years that we conducted in 2003, during the downturn, all but a handful wanted professional guidance and the desire to work with an advisor who specialized in affluent clients was even more pronounced (Exhibit 2.3).

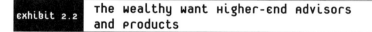

| exhibit 2.2 | The wealthy want Higher-end advisors and products |

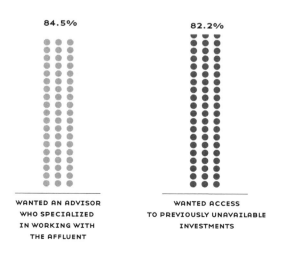

84.5%   82.2%

WANTED AN ADVISOR
WHO SPECIALIZED
IN WORKING WITH
THE AFFLUENT

WANTED ACCESS
TO PREVIOUSLY UNAVAILABLE
INVESTMENTS

n = 388 inheritors.
source: prince & associates, 2000.

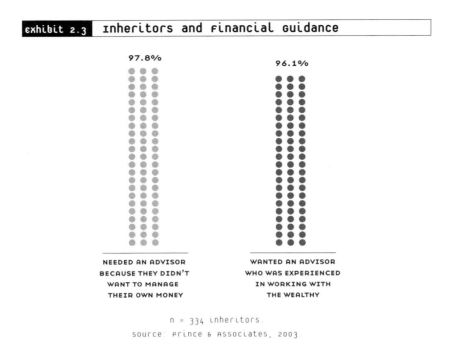

exhibit 2.3   **Inheritors and Financial Guidance**

97.8%

96.1%

NEEDED AN ADVISOR
BECAUSE THEY DIDN'T
WANT TO MANAGE
THEIR OWN MONEY

WANTED AN ADVISOR
WHO WAS EXPERIENCED
IN WORKING WITH
THE WEALTHY

n = 334 Inheritors.
source: Prince & Associates, 2003

Not surprisingly, more than half of those inheritors in the first study, 55.2%, switched their primary advisor after inheriting money. By the time of the second study in 2003, the percentage had risen to an ominous 79.6%.

¡ Manage It "with me," Not "for me"

The bear market of 2000-2003 only reinforced the desire for professional guidance. According to the 2003 Merrill Lynch Cap Gemini Ernst & Young World Wealth Report, affluent investors "developed an inflated sense of investor self-confidence that led to self-directed, high-risk investment choices" during the long bull market. But when the bear market arrived and lingered, "The fear of navigating alone compelled high-net-worth individuals to build upon their basic investment knowledge with additional professional guidance and knowledge." The report characterized those investors as "involved, sophisticated, and savvy, but even more doubtful of their self-investment abilities."

And, supporting our argument of the relevance of wealth management, those affluent investors were looking for more than just investment advice. According to the report, 85% of high-net-worth investors, defined in the report as people with at least $1 million in investable assets, "demand comprehensive planning and advisory capabilities from their providers, a notable increase from previous years."

The increased demand for guidance, however, "was not indicative of a return to the pre-1990's 'manage it for me' approach. Rather high-net-worth individuals looked for advisors who took a 'manage it with me' approach, characterized by collaboration, transparency, reliability, and high service levels." In short, they wanted wealth managers.

ı It's All About the Relationship

That need for the human touch on the part of the wealthy stems from a feeling that their financial affairs are far too complex to be managed online, but it also makes sense when one considers the main reason that affluent investors leave their advisors. Though investment expertise is a key draw for advisors when landing clients, disappointing investment performance is rarely the main reason investors move on. Again and again, our research has shown that investors leave advisors because of a poor relationship, not poor performance.

In one study we conducted in 1998 of 352 millionaires with an average of more than $10 million in investable assets, the leading cause for having switched advisors, cited by 83.8% of the respondents, was interpersonal considerations. In a 2002 study of 123 high-net-worth investors with investable assets of $500,000 or more, investors whose portfolio had been battered for better than two years, the reasons were essentially the same (Exhibit 2.4).

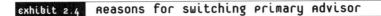

exhibit 2.4 Reasons for switching primary Advisor

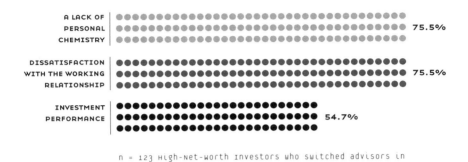

A LACK OF PERSONAL CHEMISTRY — 75.5%

DISSATISFACTION WITH THE WORKING RELATIONSHIP — 75.5%

INVESTMENT PERFORMANCE — 54.7%

n = 123 High-Net-worth Investors who switched advisors in the preceding year. Source: Prince & Associates, 2002.

While it's clear that a lack of rapport between wealthy clients and their advisors is often the principal reason for clients switching advisors, the importance of superior investment performance can't be discounted. Year after year of weak investment performance will swamp the best relationship management strategies. At the same time, some wealthy clients are willing to overlook an advisor's limited interpersonal skills – the inability to return phone calls or explain a strategy, for instance – if the advisor is beating the market and his or her peers again and again. Still, it's our contention that most financial advisors can better control the nature of their client relationships than investment returns.

ı Wanted: An Advisory Team Manager

Our research has also shown that the affluent usually have more than one financial advisor working for them, which makes sense given how many products, services, and issues have to be managed. In our studies, investors with more than $1 million in investable assets have anywhere from three to six advisors who provide a range of interconnected services. They've taken the lesson of diversification to heart and are no more likely to put all of their assets with one advisor than they are to invest in just one stock. Clients are hedging their bets – and spreading their assets – as they did after the Depression when they were loathe to leave all of their savings in one place and instead scattered them among a dozen banks and their mattress.

The team approach has a number of ramifications. First, no advisor is operating in a vacuum; each is continually being measured against the client's other advisors. And they aren't being compared on the basis of their professional expertise alone – you can't easily measure investment advice against insurance advice, for instance – but rather on the quality of the relationship.

Secondly, with a team of advisors in place, there will be a need for a team leader, a personal CFO so to speak. The financial advisor who's best at maintaining a relationship and living up to the client's expectations while being able to coordinate the experts on the client's behalf goes to the front of the line for more assets as well as referrals. The advisor who's the wealth manager is in charge of the client's team and stands to benefit from being the conduit for products and services that the client would have previously obtained directly from other advisors.

When executed properly, bringing in a team will not eat into your share of wallet but increase it. If that team is in-house, it's there to support you, not siphon income away. And if it's an outside team of specialists, the odds are that the services that you're bringing them in for aren't ones that you previously offered in any case. In other words, while you may have to split fees in some cases, it is for services and products that were not previously providing you with any income at all. And 1% of something is clearly better than 100% of nothing.

ı A Diverse Group with some common Goals

The combination of money, involvement, information, and dependence has helped shape today's affluent investors. And the new affluent are a disparate group. Some formed their own companies. Others quietly became millionaires through years of hard work and savings. Still others inherited a bundle. For the financial advisors looking to work with these high-net-worth investors as well as the established affluent, however, there are some common threads beyond the wealth.

First, the new affluent are interested in products and services expressly designed for the wealthy. Once they become "aware" of their affluence, the old products and services – and often their old financial advisors – are usually not enough. They expect the perks of affluence to include a new slate of options and a relationship with an advisor who understands how to handle wealth and the wealthy.

Second, the new affluent by and large want a centralized and simplified financial life. There are simply too many choices and scenarios for all but a handful of affluent investors to stay on top of. They want to be informed and, to varying degrees, involved, but they do not want a second career as a financial professional.

Finally, they want help from financial advisors, including lead advisors who fill the role of wealth manager. The affluent understand the value of advice and perspective. They want someone to serve as the chief financial officer to their chief executive officer. That's where you come in.

Naturally, there are lots of people vying to fill that role of personal CFO. There are accountants who offer advanced planning, brokers who sell insurance, lawyers who deliver investment advice. Those shifting roles show how profoundly the field has changed – and how wide open it is.

The result is a new advisory model for affluent investors that entails delivering a comprehensive and highly customized package of financial and planning options with a deep under-standing nurtured by contact and connection. And there's a new opportunity for the advisors who can deliver on the promise of this model by becoming – and positioning themselves as – wealth managers.

case study

spreading the wealth

Ted, a physician, developed and patented a surgical instrument and medical procedure which were later exchanged to a publicly-traded company for a large block of stock. Because Ted didn't want to risk having all of his wealth tied up in one stock, his wealth manager hedged the stock position, obtained an 80% loan, and put the money in a fund of funds. The wealth manager also coordinated a team of specialists to develop an asset protection plan. In so doing, the team uncovered a number of estate issues that, in turn, led to the sale of a life insurance policy that would eventually cover Ted's estate taxes.

self-diagnostic

▮ Reviewing Industry Trends

How would you rate the impact of each of the following industry trends on your practice today? use the following scale and also specify whether this impact has been positive or negative for your practice.

little or no impact   *considerable impact*

`< 1   2   3   4   5   6   7   8   9   10 >`

	impact	positive	negative
▮ THE INCREASE IN THE NUMBER OF MILLIONAIRES	☐	☐	☐
▮ THE DOWNTURN IN THE STOCK MARKET	☐	☐	☐
▮ INCREASED AVAILABILITY OF INFORMATION FOR INVESTORS	☐	☐	☐
▮ THE GREATER COMPLEXITY OF YOUR CLIENTS' FINANCIAL AFFAIRS	☐	☐	☐
▮ INCREASED INVOLVEMENT BY YOUR CLIENTS IN THEIR OWN FINANCIAL AFFAIRS	☐	☐	☐
▮ THE DESIRE AMONG THE AFFLUENT FOR A CONSULTATIVE RELATIONSHIP	☐	☐	☐
TOTAL	☐	☐	☐

A wealth manager would have a score of **48** or more where each of the trends is seen as positive.

All of these trends strongly enhance the ability of wealth managers to be more successful in the following ways:

- **The increase in the number of millionaires.** The benefit of this trend is straightforward: the more wealthy people there are, the more prospective clients there are.

- **The downturn in the stock market.** When the stock market was booming, everyone was an investment genius. The bursting of the equity bubble has, more than ever, made high-net-worth investors realize that they need to turn to qualified financial advisors – and they need to be broadly diversified, a strategy that those advisors can help them execute. Furthermore, the downturn has, and will continue to, thin the ranks of financial advisors, enabling the better ones to dominate the business.

- **Increased availability of information for investors.** Information and knowledge are very different, and the affluent want financial advisors who can convert raw information into actionable insights.

- **Greater complexity of financial affairs.** The more complex the client's financial affairs, the more they need a financial advisor who can bring everything together for them. They prefer a financial advisor who can manage the many financial (and related) issues they are confronted with and then provide a variety of solutions. That financial advisor is a wealth manager.

- **Increased involvement by your clients in their own financial affairs.** Because wealth managers are drawing on a network of advisors and a broad array of products and services, they're able to offer alternative solutions that their affluent clients can compare and consider.

- **The rise of the consultative relationship among the affluent.** The wealthy want a highly interactive relationship focused on addressing their evolving financial concerns, and the wealth management model is premised on contact and connection.

why wealth management matters

we've now established why wealth management matters to high-net-worth clients: they get a streamlined financial life; they get access to all of the products and services especially designed for, and exclusively available to, the affluent; and, on the interpersonal level, they get a more consultative working relationship with their primary advisor.

Now it's time to further address why wealth management should matter to you, to justify why you'd do the work it takes to move to the wealth management model. In this case, the answer is concise: more money.

▎circumstantial evidence Abounds

For anyone in the advisory industry, there's plenty of circumstantial evidence for the profit potential of wealth management. First, there are the legions of advisors who've restyled themselves as wealth managers. And then there are the many financial services firms that have dramatically expanded their wealth management capability by either beefing up an existing entity, starting a new one, or acquiring a firm that already had a reputation for working with the affluent, as was the case with Schwab buying the white-shoe US Trust. But becoming a wealth manager is not the same as succeeding as one. That's why, when making the case for wealth management, there's no better proof of its viability than the bottom line.

To make that case, we'll first consider what financial advisors see as their greatest business challenges. We'll then reaffirm the value of client contact and show how it leads directly to more assets under management and more referrals. Next, we'll cite research that demonstrates how financial services businesses have made more money by adopting the wealth management model. Finally, we'll see how wealth managers decisively out-earned their counterparts in brokerage and investments during the downturn that followed the bursting of the equity bubble in 2000.

| The top two challenges

In 2002, we conducted a state-of-the-industry survey that involved 4,106 advisors. Among many other questions, we asked them to list the biggest business challenges, and the top two answers were 1) finding affluent clients and 2) generating significant asset growth (Exhibit 3.1). No surprise there, but it's important to emphasize again the link between the two: To succeed at a higher level, advisors must have clients who are affluent enough to make the implementation of wealth management logical; and to get those clients – and enjoy that profitability – it's our contention that many advisors would be well served by becoming wealth managers.

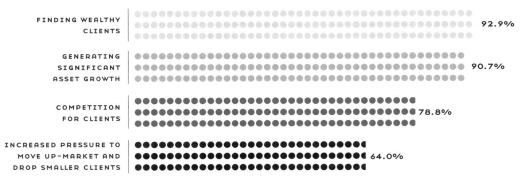

n = 4,106 financial advisors. Source: Prince & Associates, 2002.

The number three challenge was the threat of competition – everyone wants to get in on the wealth management business, of course, and in Chapter 4 we will explore how advisors can differentiate themselves from their peers. Finally, almost two-thirds of the respondents cited the need to drop their less-affluent (or less-profitable clients) and focus on the ones with the greatest profit potential. In Chapter 7, we will consider ways to assess client value and strategies for transitioning clients to other advisors.

Interestingly, when we narrowed our pool of respondents to the 391 most successful financial advisors (the 9.5% who focus on the affluent), asset growth was not at the top of the list of challenges (Exhibit 3.2). For those top advisors, success and profitability hinged on finding and keeping affluent clients.

exhibit 3.2   challenges confronting High-Net-worth
                financial advisors

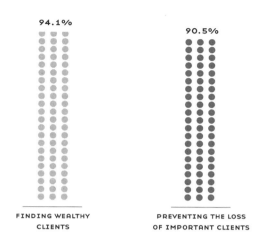

94.1%

90.5%

FINDING WEALTHY
CLIENTS

PREVENTING THE LOSS
OF IMPORTANT CLIENTS

n = 391 financial advisors
source: Prince & Associates, 2002

ı not just existing clients

Because wealth managers are positioned to draw on the full spectrum
of products and services from the fields of brokerage, investment
management, and advanced planning, they're able to provide more
sophisticated financial solutions to existing clients. These more
sophisticated financial solutions help clients achieve their
agendas and enable the wealth manager to profit in myriad ways.

ı The Power of Referrals

At the same time, the ability to summon such broad expertise allows you to move beyond your current clientele. Indeed, the wealth management model lends itself to the cultivation of new clients because it's solutions-based and client-centric as opposed to being narrowly focused on products and investments.

As we all know, the best way to generate a steady flow of new affluent clients is through referrals, either from other affluent clients or the attorneys and accountants who work with them.

With respect to client referrals, the wealth management model can help because:

I The consultative nature of the relationship leads to an interpersonal bond that makes it easier to learn about – and relate to – the client's friends and business associates.

I When clients understand the broader array of products and services that's available under the wealth management umbrella, they'll think of more people they know who can benefit from that array.

In the wealth management arena in particular, it can be just as important to promote yourself to other high-end advisors as it is to affluent clients. For centers of influence, the accountants and attorneys who work with the affluent, the broader wealth management model is more attractive than the limited financial advisory model; simply stated, when you have more solutions to offer to your clients and fellow advisors, they'll have more clients to refer.

In addition, the more you can educate accountants and attorneys about your capabilities, the more often you'll be the wealth manager they turn to with their referrals. Taking the time to understand their business model and sharing your practice management and marketing know-how can only strengthen your case (for more on positioning yourself with clients and fellow advisors, see Chapter 4).

ı client contact ıs decisive

Finding high-net-worth clients is the top challenge for financial advisors and, as noted in Chapter 1, a consultative connection is the cornerstone when it comes to building wealth management relationships with those clients. For affluent clients, indeed for all clients, regular and meaningful interaction – phone conversations, face-to-face meetings, even emails – is among the most important elements of any consultative relationship. And, in our extensive research among high-net-worth investors and their advisors, we've repeatedly found that those clients who've been regularly contacted and communicated with by understanding advisors are predisposed to give those advisors more money to manage, to provide referrals, and to stay with them.

A 2002 research study of 191 investors with at least $500,000 in investable assets once again validated the value of contact. Those advisors who took the time to set and adhere to contact parameters with their clients were six times more likely to get additional assets to manage within a six-month time frame than those who did not. And the fact that only 31 of the 191 investors were getting what they wanted shows just how wide open the wealth management field continues to be.

A 2001 study of 313 investors with more than $1 million in investable assets was similarly persuasive when it came to the power of contact (Exhibit 3.3). Nearly half of the clients who'd been called by their advisors in the preceding six months were likely to give that advisor more assets and referrals. In contrast, not one of the clients who had not been called was considering doing so.

| exhibit 3.3 | The value of contacting clients |

n = 313 high-net-worth clients. source: Prince & Associates, 2001.

The above examples don't even address what happens when clients are in a heightened state of anxiety and more likely to blame or change their advisors (Exhibit 3.4). In separate studies conducted among affluent investors after a market correction in 1997, on the heels of a hyper-volatile day for the stock market in 2000, in the wake of the terrorist attack on the United States in September 2001, and in the midst of the seemingly unending downturn in 2000-2003, the story was the same: proactive client connection led directly to more assets to manage and more referrals.

| exhibit 3.4 | client contact During Tense Times |

| contact and the market correction of october 24-27, 1997

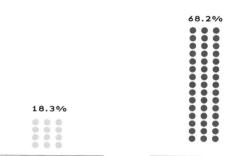

68.2%

18.3%

ADVISORS WHO CALLED
THEIR AFFLUENT CLIENTS

ADVISORS WHO CALLED THEIR
CLIENTS DURING THE CORRECTION
WERE GIVEN AN AVERAGE OF
$260,000 IN ADDITIONAL
ASSETS TO MANAGE

n = 349 advisors. source: prince & Associates, 1997.

| contact and the volatility of April 4, 2000

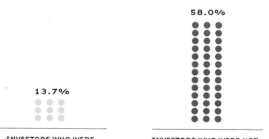

58.0%

13.7%

INVESTORS WHO WERE
CONTACTED BY THEIR
ADVISORS

INVESTORS WHO WERE NOT
CONTACTED AND SAID THEY PLANNED
TO MOVE ASSETS AWAY FROM
THEIR FINANCIAL ADVISOR

n = 1,467 clients. source: prince & Associates, 2000.

▌contact and the terrorist attack of september 11, 2001

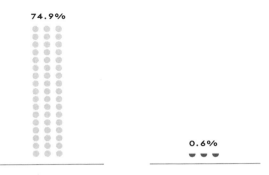

74.9%

0.6%

CLIENTS CONTACTED WHO
WERE "LIKELY" TO MOVE MORE
ASSETS TO THEIR ADVISOR

CLIENTS NOT CONTACTED
WHO WERE "LIKELY"
TO MOVE MORE ASSETS TO
THEIR ADVISOR

n = 216 clients. source: prince & associates, 2001.

▌contact during the downturn of 2000-2003

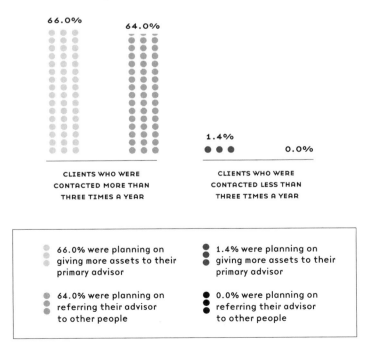

66.0%

64.0%

1.4%   **0.0%**

CLIENTS WHO WERE
CONTACTED MORE THAN
THREE TIMES A YEAR

CLIENTS WHO WERE
CONTACTED LESS THAN
THREE TIMES A YEAR

66.0% were planning on
giving more assets to their
primary advisor

1.4% were planning on
giving more assets to their
primary advisor

64.0% were planning on
referring their advisor
to other people

0.0% were planning on
referring their advisor
to other people

n = 244 clients. source: prince & associates, 2002.

ı contact and content

As vital as client contact is to affluent clients, it's also important to remember that the nature of that contact – what you talk about – is meaningful. Our research has shown that affluent clients aren't interested in having products pushed on them. They're interested in conversations and suggestions that speak to their long-term financial well-being. They want to talk, share their experiences, be reassured. They also want their advisor to connect with them on a personal level. In a survey we conducted asking what advisors and their affluent clients talked about after the tragedy of 9.11, for instance, the answer was not investments but, roundly speaking, life. Here were the top topics of conversation (Exhibit 3.5):

exhibit 3.5	what clients and advisors talked about after 9.11

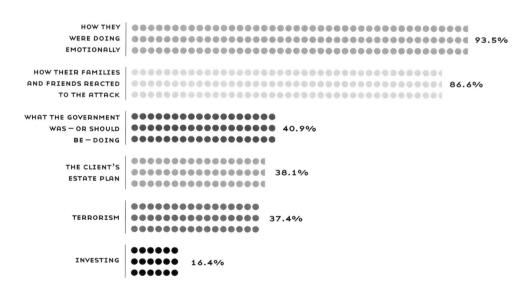

n = 216 clients. source: prince & associates, 2001.

Three studies of a total of 754 investors with a least $1 million in investable assets conducted during the stock market downturn of 2000-2002 also uncovered some interesting trends in the nature of the client/advisor relationship. As losses mounted, the affluent investors were far less receptive to ideas from their advisors, much more cautious about investing in general, and far more tax-sensitive. Further, the number of affluent investors who fired one or more of their advisors rose from 0.3% in 2000 to 16.5% in 2002. Over the same period, the number of investors who rated the overall quality of their primary advisor as "very" or "extremely" good declined from 70.4% to 39.6%. The average number of advisors per investor, however, rose from 2.4 to 3.5 during that time. In short, though the affluent were subjecting their advisors to closer scrutiny, they were nonetheless steadily increasing the size of their advisory team.

ı The wealth management edge

Contact and connection are the foundation of any consultative relationship – and the cornerstone of wealth management and advisor profitability. Now it's time to see how wealth management products and services delivered within the context of a consultative relationship can pay off.

To do that, we analyzed two types of financial services providers that had adopted the wealth management model to varying degrees: private banking and life insurance.

Private banking departments have traditionally delivered banking, credit, trust, and investment services to affluent clients. At first glance that may seem like wealth management, but it's not wealth management as we have defined it because advanced planning isn't part of the package. However, a few private banks have made the move to full-scale wealth management, including the advanced planning component. So how have they fared? Has wealth management proved to be more profitable than traditional banking?

To find out, we conducted a survey of 98 private banks. In these banks, the minimum account size was $500,000 in liquid assets. Our first finding was that there was not one service model but three:

⎮ **Basic**: These private banks provided investment management and trust services as well as traditional banking services.

⎮ **enhanced**: These banks offered the Basic model as well as credit.

⎮ **comprehensive**: These private banks offered all of the services listed above as well as advanced planning.

About half of the banks in the study, 46, offered their clients the Basic wealth management model, 29 were in the Enhanced category, and the other 23 were Comprehensive (Exhibit 3.6). This breakdown is in keeping with our observation that even though private banks had incorporated wealth management in some form, very few had implemented a complete, planning-driven wealth management model.

exhibit 3.6 The Business Models of Private Banks

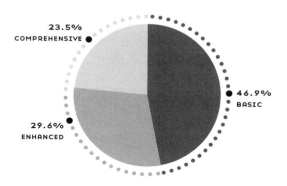

23.5% COMPREHENSIVE

46.9% BASIC

29.6% ENHANCED

Using the profitability numbers from the banks in each group, we built analytical models that allowed us to financially compare the three types of business models that the private banks offered. We statistically controlled for variables such as the wealth of the clientele and how long they had been customers of the bank. This methodology enabled us to compare the private banks in an apples-to-apples manner.

In order to illustrate the profit variances, we created an index by setting the base profitability of the bank group with the Basic model at $1,000. Private banks that had implemented the Enhanced menu of services earned significantly more, or $1,134 on the index. Finally, private banks with the Comprehensive wealth management model more than doubled the profitability of the Basic version (Exhibit 3.7).

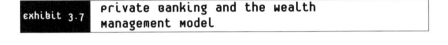

exhibit 3.7	private Banking and the wealth Management Model

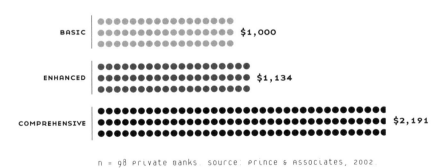

n = 98 private Banks. Source: prince & Associates, 2002.

The conclusion is inarguable: For private banks, the ability to offer affluent clients a broader platform of expertise resulted in greater profitability.

ı wealth management and Life Insurance

Life insurance is already an important element of wealth management because of its use in estate planning. As a result, in order to sell life insurance, life insurance agents often market and provide planning services. And like private banking, the life insurance industry is moving toward wealth management on other fronts by progressing beyond its core competency and offering investment management and related advisory services.

In order to assess the progress of wealth management in the insurance industry, we examined 266 life insurance agents who provided wealth transfer planning services. The sample included two groups of 133 life insurance agents who had annual incomes of between $75,000 and $100,000 from selling life insurance. The first group, Life Only, sold life insurance and provided wealth transfer planning services. The second group, Life + Investments, offered life insurance, wealth transfer services, and also fee-based asset management services in forms such as a mutual fund wrap or managed account. As you can see by Exhibit 3.8, those agents in the Life+ Investments group were able to increase their annual income by 16.1% over the two-year time frame and also increase the amount of life insurance they sold. Further, the Life+ Investments group was well-positioned to generate greater annuity-type revenues. That is, they'll continue to collect investment advisory fees without necessarily having to make another sale. Once again, the nearer an advisor, in this case a life insurance agent, moves toward wealth management, the more money he or she stands to make.

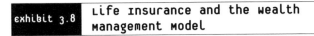

exhibit 3.8	Life Insurance and the Wealth Management Model

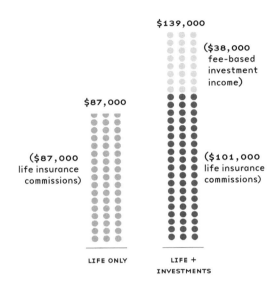

$139,000

($38,000 fee-based investment income)

$87,000

($87,000 life insurance commissions)

($101,000 life insurance commissions)

LIFE ONLY

LIFE + INVESTMENTS

n = 266 Life Insurance agents.
source: Prince & Associates, 2002.

▮ Three Business Models

Like private bankers and life insurance agents, some financial advisors have adopted wealth management and some are sticking to a more traditional business model. To see how the various business models were faring, we took the same group of 4,106 financial advisors cited earlier and, based on the way they described their practices, we divided them into three broad categories. While every advisor's practice is in some ways unique, they did cluster into the following three sub-groups:

- **Investment Generalists**: Advisors who provide a wide range of investments but don't have a financial planning orientation.

- **Product Specialists**: Advisors who are focused on an investment niche such as managed accounts, 144 stock, or fixed income, but without a planning orientation.

- **Wealth Managers**: Advisors who have adopted the holistic approach to working with clients that takes into account both sides of the client's personal P&L equation. With a strong planning orientation, the wealth manager is capable of implementing recommendations by cross-selling services and products.

Of the advisors in our study, nearly two-thirds, 2,689 out of 4,106, were Investment Generalists, and another 912 were Product Specialists. The Wealth Managers made up the smallest sub-group with only 505 (Exhibit 3.9).

exhibit 3.9 The Business Models of advisors

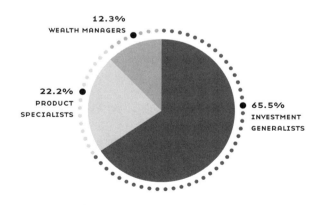

n = 4,106 Financial advisors.
source: Prince & Associates, 2002.

ı Life During a Downturn

Having established the sub-groups, we then wanted to know how each of them fared during 2001, a difficult year during which the Dow was down 7.1%, the S&P 500 fell 13.0%, and the Nasdaq dropped 21.1%. Not surprisingly, life was no easier for our 4,106 financial advisors and, as a group, their revenues were off 34.0% during 2001. But Wealth Managers, as Exhibit 3.10 illustrates, actually increased their revenues during 2001, an improvement that stands in stark contrast to the performance of Investment Generalists, whose business was off by more than half. The Wealth Managers were able to outperform their fellow financial advisors during the downturn by capitalizing on the built-in attributes of the business model, including the ability to leverage client relationships, to cross-sell, and to provide products and services not linked to the performance of the stock market. The Investment Generalists, to their detriment, did not have many options when the stock market headed south and stayed there.

Product Specialists did better than Investment Generalists, but not as well as the Wealth Managers. And while the annualized production for each product specialist was down 9.4%, there was an enormous spread ranging from –89.6% to +72.1%. This range was a function of their particular product expertise and whether or not their specialty was hot – principal protected funds are a good example. In fact, because financial products cycle in and out of fashion so quickly, the Product Specialist model is most susceptible to highs and lows.

exhibit 3.10	production in 2001 by business model

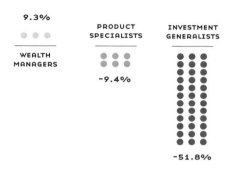

n = 4,106 financial advisors.
source= prince & associates, 2002.

ı The upper crust

We then further narrowed the group to the 391 financial advisors at the highest end of the revenue curve, those who made more than $400,000 a year, and, as Exhibit 3.11 shows, the trend was even more pronounced.

exhibit 3.11 High-end Production in 2001 by Business Model

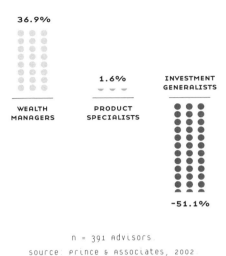

n = 391 Advisors.
source: Prince & Associates, 2002.

Even when working with high-net-worth clients, the revenues of Investment Generalists fell by more than half. Product Specialists broke just above even but, again, it was the Wealth Managers who easily outdistanced the rest of the field, with revenues increasing by more than one-third.

The revenues of Wealth Managers held up through the downturn because the wealth management model generated profits for services such as life insurance or asset protection planning. That's particularly relevant today because, in the wake of the recession, investor confidence remains fragile, and those financial advisors who can move their business model away from being totally dependent on the stock market can at least in part protect themselves – and their clients – from further fluctuations.

To recap, whether we're considering private bankers, life insurance agents, or financial advisors, the result of embracing wealth management was the same: financial success.

Life After Work

Making money with the wealth management model doesn't solely depend on your getting new affluent clients; it can also lead to increased profitability from your existing clients. Most of Louise's money was tied up in the family business so there was little in the way of investable assets for her financial advisor to manage. Because her health was poor, she wanted to take out a life insurance policy that would benefit her nieces and nephews. She also wanted to monetize a portion of her holdings in the family business so she could see the world. Finally, she wanted to be sure that her estate could cover her death taxes. While a financial advisor might have only seen a dearth of investable assets, a wealth manager, drawing on an array of experts, converted the business into an Employee Stock Ownership Plan (ESOP). By doing so, the family would maintain control while Louise acquired stock, hedged the stock, took a loan against the hedged position to purchase life insurance to cover her estate taxes, and ended up with millions that needed to be invested.

self-diagnostic

∎ Appraising Business Models

use the following scale to rate how concerned you are
about each of the following:

not at all a concern   *a very significant concern*

‹ 1   2   3   4   5   6   7   8   9   10 ›

∎ **FINDING WEALTHY CLIENTS**

∎ **GENERATING SIGNIFICANT ASSET GROWTH**

∎ **COMPETITION FOR CLIENTS**

∎ **INCREASED PRESSURE TO MOVE UP-MARKET AND**
  DROP SMALLER CLIENTS

∎ **PREVENTING THE LOSS OF WEALTHY CLIENTS**

TOTAL

A score of **25** or higher indicates that you need to take action.
Keep in mind that the move to wealth management isn't a sure-fire
cure or the only business model that can ameliorate these concerns.
However, as we've demonstrated, it's been highly effective in
helping advisors acquire wealthy clients and their investable assets.
(In Chapter 7, we'll see how to transition those clients who stand
to be less profitable for you over the long term.)

Now that you have a feel for wealth management, take a moment
and write down your top two business concerns from the above list as
seen in the context of all three dominant business models — Wealth
Manager, Product Specialist, and Investment Generalist. In addition,
detail the ways in which you think each model can help you overcome
these concerns. While you may well find that your concerns are the
same in each case, based on what we have discussed so far, the
wealth management model is best suited to address them.

wealth manager

CONCERNS	SOLUTION
1.	
2.	

product specialist

CONCERNS	SOLUTION
1.	
2.	

investment generalist

CONCERNS	SOLUTION
1.	
2.	

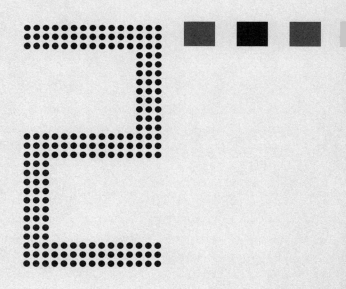

thinking and acting like a wealth manager

- A NEW MINDSET, A BIGGER PICTURE
- WEALTH MANAGERS COMPARED WITH FINANCIAL ADVISORS
- REMEMBER YOUR STRENGTHS
- GETTING TO KNOW YOUR CLIENTS
- POSITIONING YOURSELF AS A WEALTH MANAGER

To move from being a financial advisor to a wealth manager requires, as we shall see in this second section of the book, a seismic shift in the way that you think, work, and interact with your clients, prospects, and fellow advisors.

We've demonstrated that the wealth management model is not only what most affluent clients prefer, but that it's also a potentially more profitable way of doing business, two pretty strong arguments in its favor. Still, there's no shortcut to success. You can't become a wealth manager simply by printing new business cards, taking an online correspondence course, or reading the back of a cereal box. And not everyone will want to accept the challenge. For some financial advisors, wealth management may not be in sync with the way they run their business, the wishes of their clients, or their skill sets and knowledge base. And for those who do want to make the move and face head-on the arduous work involved, the first step may well be the most challenging: convincing yourself that you're capable of being a wealth manager.

More Than Investable Assets

To understand the professional and psychic ground that has to be traversed on the way to becoming a wealth manager, we should first compare the major characteristics of financial advisors with those of wealth managers (Exhibit 4.1).

exhibit 4.1 Wealth Managers vs. Financial Advisors	
Financial Advisor orientation	Wealth Management orientation
Focus on specific products.	Focus on financial solutions.
Assessment tied to products offered.	Holistic assessment of client's financial needs.
Focus on, and knowledge of, a limited menu of products and services.	Broader menu of financial products and services.
Limited consideration of the interrelationship of financial products and services.	Ability to manage the inter-relationship of various financial products and services.
Primarily works alone.	Brings together and manages advisory team to best serve the client.

Products vs. Solutions

The first point of differentiation – that financial advisors sell specific products while wealth managers promote financial solutions – may have by now been heard often enough to seem like a cliché, but it concisely embodies the fundamental difference between the two business models. A financial advisor may offer a variety of products such as the latest mutual fund, the hottest stock, or access to a highly regarded money manager. But each product is principally investment-oriented and is a stand-alone, one-time sale, even in the case of fee-based money management that's primarily driven by the product's money management attributes and the client's level of investable assets.

For wealth managers, the client's long-range financial goals and needs, as determined by an informed and up-to-date client profile, lead to the choice of product. And while it may well be an investment option, the product will not be selected and promoted solely on the basis of the client's investable assets or portfolio mix. In short, the product is subsidiary to the plan.

This represents an entirely different way of going about – and thinking about – a relationship. But once you understand a client as a whole person rather than simply an investor, the assets, as well as other opportunities, will follow. And all of this is very much in keeping with the survey results that we've already cited showing that the great majority of clients value the relationship with their advisor over investment returns.

It should also be reiterated that no one advisor is going to manage 100% of a client's assets. Even before the current downturn made investors skittish about putting all of their assets in one place, they preferred to have a range of advisors just as they have a range of investment vehicles. But there is wiggle room: Each advisor can get a few more percentage points of the client's total assets (or, conversely, lose a few) based on the nature and quality of the relationship. And among affluent clients, each percentage point of wealth gained can add up very nicely over the long term.

There's one other important aspect of wealth management to remember:

> | It's far easier to exert control over a relationship than it is over investments; even the most astute money manager can't outmaneuver a recession.

All of this, of course, relates to the different compensation models of wealth managers and financial advisors that we considered in Chapter 1. The wealth management model, remember, has the profound benefit of having four potential income streams: advisory fees, commissions, asset-based fees, and performance fees. The wealth manager, unlike the financial advisor, does not have to sell a product to make money, which in itself begins to shift the advisor/client dynamic. The wealth manager is seen as less of a salesperson – less of a product pusher – and more of a consultant. Selling is driven by the needs of the client.

ı The point of the product

Now let's take that first distinction, the focus on specific products, a step further. When a financial advisor recommends a product, he or she will lead with the product's benefits – why that product in particular works for the client; why, for instance, an index fund makes sense. Furthermore, the product will usually be promoted and sold separately; it's not part of a holistic package.

A wealth manager, in contrast, has an informed view of the client's total financial picture, as well as a better understanding of his or her goals and limitations, and that understanding will dictate which products come into play. As such, a product will be positioned, not promoted, as the next logical step in an ongoing plan to meet the client's long-term agenda. Along the way, you'll engender trust by putting your client's needs and wants over a given product.

ı A Longer Menu

Because the products that a financial advisor promotes have a somewhat limited scope – they'll usually revolve around investments – there's a finite number of options to choose from. Wealth managers can offer their clients the same investment choices (though positioned in a different way) and can also offer products and services that are not necessarily investment oriented, notably advanced planning options.

Wealth managers can deliver so many products and services because they've cultivated a relationship whereby any of them may be appropriate at a given moment. They have a richer understanding of each client's personal and financial life that gives them more options to choose from. Importantly, clients are aware that you know them (and do not need to push any one product or service), which in turn makes them far more receptive to what you have to offer.

Again, in order to manage the complex financial lives of affluent clients, the ability to draw upon a wide array of services and products is critical. Moreover, wealth managers can combine various products and services as in the case of a customized version of private placement life insurance.

▌ An Integrated Package

It's not enough, however, to simply be able to offer a longer menu of products and services. Anyone would rightly be suspicious of a restaurant that claimed to specialize in Thai, Italian, French, and Japanese cuisines. So it would be with a wealth manager who claimed to be a master of every aspect of money management and advanced planning.

The financial advisor is not usually obliged to explain, in anything other than the most superficial way, how a product or service might fit into the bigger picture, for example, how a growth stock might round out a portfolio heavily weighted in value stocks. To a certain extent, it's a one-dimensional relationship.

For a wealth manager, the relationship is far more intricate. Each product and service has to be carefully placed in the context of the client's overall financial plan. As we shall see, it also has to be made clear that you aren't trying to be all things to your clients; one of your strengths is your access to a trusted network of experts who you call in on an as-needed basis. The prime focus is the interplay of products and services and the way they can be integrated to address a client's complete financial equation over the course of a long and mutually beneficial relationship. Having to put every product or service in perspective is clearly more challenging and time consuming, but it improves the relationship while opening the door to more potential sources of recurring revenue.

ı The wealth Management Team

The final difference between financial advisors and wealth managers relates to the way they work. Financial advisors, focusing on investments, tend to work by themselves. They're not prone to bring in a second voice or opinion – nor are they expected to. The wealth manager, with a far broader view of the client's financial needs, should have access to more products and services, as we have seen. But that doesn't mean you're expected to evolve overnight from a broker into a financial jack of all trades. A radical transformation like that, besides being well-nigh impossible to make, would also leave your clients suspicious or nervous. That's why one of the wealth manager's most important roles is to assemble an expert advisory network, the team of specialists who can be called upon for their perspective and expertise on a case-by-case basis.

As the client's CFO, you must know who to summon and when, and must also coordinate the lawyers, money managers, accountants, insurance agents, trust officers, bankers, and other advisors (for more on managing an advisory team, see Chapter 6: The Wealth

Management Team). In sum, as a wealth manager, you must have a different mindset, a grasp of the bigger picture, and the advisory resources to meet any client need.

∣ Accentuate the Positive

Along the same lines, we should note that becoming a wealth manager doesn't mean you should abandon what you do best, the strength that may have attracted the client in the first place, whether it's something as broad as picking stocks or as focused as managing concentrated stock positions. That would be folly. As noted, you're not expected to become an authority on every aspect of wealth management. Further, between concentrating on your core strength, interacting with clients, and managing an advisory network, there's already plenty for you to do without trying to master all of the many details of wealth management. You are, however, expected to have a working knowledge of each client's financial life, what you can and can't do yourself, and to know when to bring in help. Importantly, a wealth manager should also know how to position that help; each specialist should be seen by the client as an integral and informed part of the advisory team, not a free agent.

∣ The Big Picture (Again)

To recast the differences between a financial advisor and a wealth manager, here are some simple axioms:

∣ **You are not a salesperson**; you are a valued consultant.

∣ **You do not need to make a sale**; you need to build the relationship.

- you do not have to focus on investable assets;
  if you learn as much as possible about each client,
  the assets will follow.

- you do not have to push a single product;
  you have to promote an ongoing course of interaction
  that will facilitate the use of a broad range of
  products and services.

- you should not try and do everything yourself;
  you should put together an expert advisory team that
  can do it all.

Learning About clients

Implicit in the difference between financial advisors and wealth managers is the idea that the latter must have a far more intimate understanding of their clients to establish a consultative relationship; they can do more for their clients because they know more about them.

Perhaps the most effective way to demonstrate the difference between financial advisors and wealth managers when it comes to their working with clients is by looking at the way they gather information. For financial advisors, there's no shortage of forms, fact finders, and questionnaires. But from the wealth management perspective, many of those tools are skewed by a narrow focus on investable assets and net worth.

The wealth manager takes a far different – and far more personal – tack. By way of example, we asked top advisors and successful wealth managers how they gathered information and what kind of questions they asked of their affluent clients. The result is the Whole Client Model™, a data-gathering tool that can influence the nature and success of a wealth management relationship.

The Whole Client Model is organized into the following six sections:

1: Goals

SAMPLE QUESTIONS:

▌ What are your personal and professional goals?

▌ What do you want (or feel obligated to do) for your spouse, children, other family members, friends, society, and the world at large?

2: Relationships

SAMPLE QUESTIONS:

▌ Which family member relationships (spouse, children, siblings, parents, etc.) are most important?

▌ What is your religious orientation (and how devout are you)?

3: Assets

SAMPLE QUESTIONS:

▌ How are your assets structured and in whose name (yours, your spouse, a corporation)?

▌ How do you make money (and how is that likely to change in the next three years)?

4: Advisors

SAMPLE QUESTIONS:

▌ Who are the other advisors you're using and what role does each advisor play?

▌ Of late, how frequently have you switched selected advisors?

5: Process

SAMPLE QUESTIONS:

▌ How many contacts are optimal each year and in what form (face-to-face, phone, email)?

▌ What security measures are you using to protect your personal and financial information?

6: Interests

SAMPLE QUESTIONS:

❚ What are your favorite activities, TV programs, movies, and sport teams? Do you have any hobbies, like pets, or travel often?

❚ Are health and fitness important (and, if so, what's your regimen)?

The Whole Client Model is a vital wealth management tool. In order to provide a broader array of financial services and products to clients, you must have a comprehensive understanding of their needs and wants explicitly as well as implicitly expressed. Only by having this comprehensive understanding will you be able to solve their financial problems and deliver the products, services, and results they're looking for.

When using the Whole Client Model, you're not just filling in a set of forms so there's a lot of flexibility as to how you might gather the affluent client's information. Some wealth managers prefer simply categorizing the material while others opt for a more visual representation of the information such as "mind mapping," a graphic representation of the six categories of the Whole Client Model. The latter approach is very advantageous when you're conducting strategic scenario sessions, the process whereby you brainstorm with fellow advisors about which services and products would be most appropriate for a specific client.

As for the timing of the Whole Client Model, there's no one right answer. Indeed, the process will probably be incremental. Even if you're able to sit down with a client or prospect for an hour or two to ask some of these questions, you'll continue to add information and flesh out the client's profile as the relationship advances. The more you learn, the more fodder you'll have for strategic scenario sessions with your advisory team.

Further, the Whole Client Model fosters the consultative perspective that's central to wealth management. In the course of developing a detailed understanding of your client as a person, you get to know each other in a more personal way that can only enhance the relationship and the client's confidence in you.

ı interaction Not interrogation

Of course, learning about the client is not just about the questions but also about the way they're asked, the manner in which the information is compiled. That process says as much about the wealth manager as the content.

Some aspiring wealth managers may think that asking personal questions is intrusive or even offensive. We disagree. In fact, assuming they respect the wealth manager and his or her intentions – an important caveat – the majority of affluent clients are quite willing to talk about themselves because they understand that data informs a wealth manager's approach to their unique situation. As a result, a deft wealth manager should be able to get the information without handing over a questionnaire or reading through the above list. They can instead educe the information, over the course of time if necessary, by engaging affluent clients in conversations about themselves, their needs, and their interests. Above all, the process should put the client at ease by taking the form of an open-ended conversation, not an interrogation.

Leading financial advisors are adept at soliciting information from the affluent, and, not surprisingly, adroit questioning is the key to their success. Here are some of the ways those questions are categorized and tips for eliciting information:

❚ questions to obtain information: The goals here are to jog the client's memory and motivate them to share. Examples: "How are your assets structured?" "How has your investment performance been over the last couple of years?" "Who do you want to inherit your business?"

❚ questions that test comprehension: When working with an affluent client, you need to be certain the client is making an informed decision. It's therefore imperative that the client fully understands the issues, the alternatives, and the implications of any decision. Questions that result in client rephrasing, interpreting, comparing, and detailing accomplish this objective. Examples (after having explained a particular product or service): "How would you see an ESOP working for you and your family business?" "Based on our discussion, do you think a hedge fund or a fund of funds works better for you (and why)?"

❚ questions that require analysis and evaluation: Rarely are client issues cut and dried. On the contrary, they're often psychological and subtle. As a result, you must tactfully help your client to analyze the situation or issue and the consequence of any actions that might be taken. Example: "Since you're not comfortable with your children inheriting all of your money at once, how would you like that money to be administered and distributed and over what timeframe?"

❚ questions that move the process forward: When it comes to generating momentum, there's considerably more value in questions as opposed to assertions because questions enable you to take the affluent client on a guided tour of self-discovery. Examples: "Now that we've reached this stage, who else should we be bringing into this conversation and making part of this decision-making process?" "When would be a good time for us to go over these alternatives?"

ı The Benefits of the whole client model

To reiterate, the Whole Client Model is central to wealth management because 1) a truly consultative relationship is hampered when you're unaware of the critical facts and issues concerning your client, and 2) by having this broad based and deep perspective you'll uncover new opportunities for your services and products.

One of the benefits of the Whole Client Model is that it will help you hold onto a client when products don't perform as anticipated. Because of the rapport that's been established, your client will most probably give you more time to make adjustments during a period of poor or under-performance than they would an advisor with whom they have a less consultative relationship (that is, an advisor who manages their assets in a limited way as opposed to managing their financial life in a holistic manner).

ı A Business Builder

Another benefit of the Whole Client Model is that it often makes it easier for you to get business in the first place. If you've ever courted a client, you've been rejected. And, like any spurned suitor, you've anguished over where you went wrong. What could you have said or done to make it work?

As a wealth manager, rejection is that much more painful because the prospect is affluent and the payoff can be far more substantial than it might have been if you were only offering investment management or brokerage services. The fact that you spend time, resources, and your expertise getting to know the prospect further heightens the disappointment.

To get an idea where advisors were falling short, in 2003 we surveyed 103 investors who had at least $5 million in investable assets. In the previous year, all of them had met with, and received proposals from, financial advisors whom they did not hire. And their reasons for not hiring should raise a red flag or two about the way advisors are prospecting among the affluent.

Of those 103 respondents, better than four out of five said the advisor didn't understand them (Exhibit 4.2). A similarly high percentage thought the advisor's investment recommendations were off the mark. Yet only a handful said that they didn't understand those recommendations, so it wasn't a matter of being baffled; they simply knew enough to realize that the recommendations weren't right for them. No matter how you slice it, this is a very poor report card.

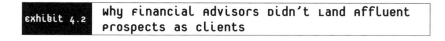

exhibit 4.2 | why financial advisors didn't land affluent prospects as clients

PROSPECTS DIDN'T FEEL UNDERSTOOD — 86.7%

PROSPECTS DIDN'T LIKE THE ADVISOR'S INVESTMENT RECOMMENDATIONS — 85.7%

PROSPECTS DIDN'T UNDERSTAND THE ADVISOR'S INVESTMENT RECOMMENDATIONS — 4.3%

n = 103 investors with at least $5 million in investable assets.
source: Prince & Associates, 2003

ı First Things First

If the majority of affluent clients aren't feeling understood, there's something very wrong with the discovery process being employed. Obviously, every affluent client wants to make a connection with the person who will handle his or her financial affairs. That understanding is a prerequisite for rapport, and, above all, trust. And if that connection isn't made at the outset, as this survey underscores, there's little hope for an ongoing relationship.

The fact that so many wealthy investors don't agree with the investment recommendations made is equally sobering. If they didn't feel understood, if their goals and unique circumstances weren't put into perspective, there was little hope for the recommendations being on target. And, looking again at the very low percentage of investors who didn't understand the recommendations, we can infer that they were sophisticated enough and sufficiently informed about their financial options to be able to accurately judge – and, in this case, reject – the recommendations.

ı Interaction at the outset
so what's an advisor to do?

First, it's important to remember once again that the discovery process with any new client is not just about assets. You have to learn as much as you can about their finances before submitting recommendations, of course. But to truly connect with prospects, it's just as important to know who they are – their goals and objectives as well as their interests and relationships – as it is to know about their portfolio holdings. That kind of personal probing, the Whole Client Model, will be less familiar territory for some advisors (and even some clients), but it makes for fertile ground when it comes to relationship building.

Furthermore, the discovery process is not a one way street: it's also an opportunity for the prospect to learn more about you and the way you do business. An essential step in developing mutual trust and understanding is helping clients know how your experience and expertise have helped similar individuals. Once they realized you've worked successfully with people like them, their confidence in your ability will increase commensurately.

| Humanizing Finances

Secondly, it's important to identify the issues that link a prospect's lifestyle and finances, especially those that have not been addressed to their satisfaction. For instance, surveys of the affluent often reveal a desire to establish a charitable legacy and instill philanthropic values in their children. But they may not have had time to articulate their values or think how those values might be best realized. And that's just one example of where the bonding process between you and a potential client can begin and where understanding can take hold.

| Make Sure You're on the Same Page

Finally, before making any recommendations, you must be sure that you understand what the affluent prospect is seeking to achieve, what complications they envision, and what concerns they have. Additionally, it's helpful to know if there are any preconceptions or interests about particular products or services that should be investigated more thoroughly or perhaps excluded from your recommendations. By reviewing these issues together, you can move toward a shared acceptance of goals and convey a level of understanding and comfort to the client that your service and your solutions will be precisely tailored to their circumstances and needs.

⎸ A client case study

Here's an example of the Whole Client Model at work. Consider the case of a wealthy 78-year-old widow in good health. Her advisor had a solid relationship with her and was managing about $5 million of her assets while only providing investment advisory services. Her advisor then made the transition to wealth management and was able to help her address a far broader array of financial issues and concerns.

By using the Whole Client Model, the advisor found that she had a total net worth of $30 million in assets, including $3 million in an IRA with an online broker. He also found that she hadn't created her own estate plan after the death of her husband, and since that time she'd become a grandmother four times over.

Her wealth manager brought in a trusts and estates lawyer to produce the required documents and make suggestions to amend and update the estate plan. In a nutshell, her goals were to leave her money to her family while mitigating estate taxes in the most cost-effective manner.

Before her wealth manager focused on the estate, her heirs stood to pay $15.5 million in estate taxes when she died plus an additional income tax of $600,000 on the IRA. To lessen the tax bite, he set up a profit-sharing plan for her and rolled the IRA she had with the online brokerage into the plan. The plan then purchased a $7 million life insurance policy, solving her estate tax issues.

The wealth transfer strategies used in this case study were not cutting-edge; the key was simply a matter of uncovering the opportunity. And by using the Whole Client Model, her wealth manager was able to get a far more in-depth understanding of the wealthy client.

| positioning yourself as a wealth manager

Even after you've convinced yourself that you can be a wealth manager, there's yet another hurdle to clear; convincing your clients, prospects, and fellow advisors.

One important element of that new positioning is the ability to recognize when it's time to summon an expert. As noted, there's nothing to be gained in being backed up by a phalanx of experts if you don't know when to call them in. In most cases, that means taking advantage of your parent firm's resources to learn more about, for instance, asset protection, wealth transfer, insurance, or charitable giving, disciplines that often fall well outside of the traditional brokerage and money management that advisors are familiar with. But the fact that you're willing to rely on an expert will in itself let clients and advisors know that you've extended your job description and client capability.

| The sound bite

Aspiring wealth managers want to be accessible and allow both prospects and potential advisory partners to get a quick read on them and their abilities. The best way to position yourself is by talking the talk; delivering a sound bite for instant client and advisor consumption.

To that end, you should have a series of tight, 30-second speeches for current clients, prospects, and other advisors, and all of them should address three key points: who you are, what you do, and who you do it for. In other words, what is your name and what company are you affiliated with; what are the products and services that you can offer and access; and who's at the receiving end of those products and services. The basic script can then be customized depending on who you're speaking with as well as their expectations and experience.

sample "sound bites"

Note: The idea is that each statement serves as a teaser that invites a return question from the prospect.

"I'm [your name] with [name of firm]. We solve financial problems for the wealthy."

"At [name of firm], our focus is on helping affluent clients achieve their dreams by providing the complete suite of wealth management solutions."

"I'm [your name] with [name of firm] and we provide a holistic wealth management approach to planning as well as cutting-edge products to successful corporate executives and business owners."

Along the way, it's important for wealth managers to not fall into the trap of promising the moon. Wealth management can be seductive in that way, but clients and advisors are going to be rightly skeptical of anyone who claims to be capable of offering an answer to every question or a solution to every problem.

reprise: why wealth management matters

After the sound bite, you have to be ready to deliver a longer sales pitch that explains why wealth management matters and support the case with scenarios and stories the prospective clients can relate to. The premise of wealth management is that today's affluent have a highly complex financial life and that many of the issues they have to deal with are interrelated; that explains the need for a holistic approach. So financial advisors looking to position themselves as wealth managers should be armed with the anecdotes and case studies that will reinforce that premise. And, whether you're meeting with a client, a prospect, or another advisor, you may want to bring in a member of your advisory team to showcase the breadth of available expertise on a particular issue.

Like the sound bite, the case studies and stories will have to be tweaked depending on whether the target is a current client, a prospect, an advisor with whom a relationship is already established, or a new advisor who's being cultivated from scratch. For the centers of influence who you have worked with before, in particular, it will be important to demonstrate that you now have access to more expertise than previously and are thus a worthy target for more wide-ranging referrals.

Positioning yourself as a wealth manager will not be an easy sell, particularly for those advisors who have rarely strayed from the familiar world of brokerage and money management. It will require some thought about your strengths and weaknesses, possibly going back to school for a crash course on an array of financial topics, and the construction of a series of thoughtful and targeted sales presentations. But, based on our research among advisors and affluent clients alike, the transition to wealth management can pay off in terms of the solidity of client relationships, increased profitability per client, and additional referrals from both clients and centers of influence such as the attorneys and accountants who work with the wealthy.

case study

Taking the sting out of taxes

Mark, a very wealthy client, was interested in investments that weren't correlated to the stock market. For a financial advisor, the solution might have been a market-neutral hedge fund, but there are constraints in this case because Mark is very sensitive to any capital gains taxes on his investments. A wealth manager would be aware of this sensitivity and be able to suggest a customized private placement variable life insurance policy to not only address Mark's concerns but also deal with his estate tax issues. Another approach would entail structuring the ownership of the hedge fund so that, like private placement variable life insurance, it was highly tax sensitive. Along the way, a wealth manager could also summon a number of experts providing support and, through the use of strategic scenario sessions, uncover other viable options such as an offshore corporation structure.

self-diagnostic

ı understanding the critical success factors

Rate the following key attributes on a scale of 1 to 10 where 1 is for an attribute that you don't have and 10 is one that you count among your core strengths.

lacking the attribute   *core strength*

‹ 1   2   3   4   5   6   7   8   9   10 ›

ı **A STRONG COMMITMENT TO DOING WHAT'S BEST
FOR YOUR CLIENTS**

ı **A CONSULTATIVE VERSUS A "PRODUCT-PUSHING" ORIENTATION**

ı **THE ABILITY TO BUILD RAPPORT WITH THE WEALTHY**

ı **A DESIRE TO ALWAYS GET BETTER AS AN ADVISOR**

ı **THE ABILITY TO WORK WELL WITH OTHER PROFESSIONALS**

TOTAL

We believe that every financial advisor needs to post a high score on this self-diagnostic whether they're striving to be wealth managers or not, but to compete in the wealth management arena, you should have a score of **40** or better.

This diagnostic is not about products or technical issues. It's about you and the skills you would need to deliver the wealth management model.

- **A strong commitment to doing what's best for your clients.** Aside from being the right course of action for many advisors, the very act of adopting and implementing the wealth management model helps foster this point of view. Indeed, your financial position is likely to be enhanced by it as well as by the fact that wealth management is not tied to just one or two products.

- **A consultative versus a "product-pushing" orientation.** By being consultative, you would be able to develop a deeper understanding of what your affluent clients need and want and then provide the appropriate services and products. In contrast, financial advisors with a "product" orientation have a limited audience.

- **The ability to build rapport with the wealthy.** Unless you can build rapport with the wealthy, you won't be successful. As noted, the consultative orientation of the wealth management model fosters rapport. That experience in relationship building will also help you cultivate new clients.

- **A desire to always get better as an advisor.** We feel this is paramount to success in the financial services industry, and it's particularly important with respect to the wealth management model. Take, for instance, the fact that a wealth manager must stay current with changing affluent market trends, regulatory changes, and state-of-the-art products and services. Unless, you're committed to always improving as a practitioner, you're going to be left behind in this fast-moving financial services environment.

- **The ability to work well with other professionals.** As we've said, it's impossible to deliver wealth management all by yourself; it's a team activity. That's why you should be prepared to establish solid working relationships, incorporate complementary skills and working styles, and clearly define roles and responsibilities for team members.

creating a wealth management platform

- A CHECKLIST OF WEALTH MANAGEMENT NEEDS
- ASSEMBLING THE RIGHT RESOURCES
- WHAT EXPERT ADVISORS SHOULD BRING TO THE TABLE
- WHERE TO FIND THE EXPERTS
- HOW TO INTERACT WITH YOUR CLIENT'S EXISTING ADVISORS
- HOW TO COMPENSATE EXPERT ADVISORS
- STAYING STATE OF THE ART

In committing to wealth management, you're
promising clients that you'll be able to deliver a full slate of
financial products and services – brokerage, investments, and
advanced planning – as well as an enhanced and across-the-board
consultative capability. In this chapter, we'll take a look at what's
on the checklist of wealth management needs, focusing in particular on the way you can find and evaluate the other advisors you'll
need to support you and your clients. Keep in mind that this is not
a static list. The desires of affluent clients, the skills of advisors,
and the range of available products and services are all evolving
and will have to be regularly reconsidered and accommodated. At
this time, however, the following are the key components:

---

exhibit 5.1 The Basic Wealth Management Checklist

Brokerage

- Bonds
- Equities
- Options
- Derivatives
- Managing concentrated stock positions

Investment Management

- Cash management
- Corporate retirement plans
- Alternative investments
- Portfolio construction and maintenance
- Managed accounts
- Mutual funds
- 529 accounts

Advanced Planning

- Estate planning
- Business transition or succession planning
- Wealth enhancement
- Asset protection
- Charitable giving

The Team Approach

The heart of the wealth management platform is the expert support structure – the network of professionals that you must have in place to fully meet the needs of affluent clients. In the best case, that platform can be the basis for providing superior service to your clients, warding off the competition, growing your business, and making money for you and your fellow advisors.

So who's on the team? There's a wide array of talents and knowledge out there to tap into. Accountants and attorneys are usually part of the network, as are insurance agents and sometimes even actuaries. A comprehensive professional network might also include a trusts and estates lawyer, a banker, a money manager or two (or three), and third-party administrators. Increasingly, management consultants, family business specialists, and even psychologists are on board. Whatever the constituency, a network that accurately reflects the interests and needs of a wealth manager's current or targeted clientele should pay dividends over time and reward each of its members.

---

exhibit 5.2 **The core wealth management team roster**

- Trusts and estates lawyer
- Life insurance specialist
- Derivatives specialist
- Securities lawyer
- Charitable giving specialist
- Valuation specialist
- Income tax specialist
- Actuary

Any such list of professional resources can be misleading, however. Complementary wealth management skills are not always where you might expect them to be. An accountant might be an expert in advanced planning, for example, and an insurance agent might be an authority on asset protection. In short, don't be taken in by titles; it's the skills you must accumulate.

An Extension Away

If you're part of a large financial services firm, many if not all of the preceding services, products, and professionals will be only a phone extension away; you'll rarely have to summon outside resources. In recent years, many of those firms have in fact heightened their pursuit of more affluent clients by beefing up their wealth management capabilities. That doesn't mean there's no work involved at your end. A wealth manager still has to oversee a network, even if it's in-house, and know who to bring in and when. In fact, running the network can be more challenging than putting it together, and the success of any network will depend as much on who's in charge as who's on board. (In the next chapter, we'll take a closer look at how wealth managers run and maintain professional networks.)

Where to Find Them

For those who don't have such ready resources, it's a very different story. You'll have to put in place a network of the individual and independent advisors who can provide all of the services, products, and knowledge that you don't already offer. There's an upside to putting together your own team, however: you'll have the pick of the advisory field and not be beholden to anyone. But you'll have to track down advisors who'll deliver the goods, accept the team concept, and reflect well upon you with your clients. So where do you start?

There are a number of effective ways to go about it. The first places to go are the financial (or other) firms that already provide you with products and services. A number of life insurance companies offer advanced planning services, for example, with an emphasis on wealth transfer and charitable giving. Similarly, money management firms provide investment consulting support. If you're successfully promoting and placing their products, they should be incented to help you out.

Along the way, depending on your business model, you may well find that you have to enter into a number of working agreements with other types of financial institutions, including life insurance companies, life insurance brokerage operations, trust institutions, and third-party administrators. Each company will have to be vetted for the quality of its products and the level of its client service capabilities. Selling agreements will need to be negotiated, and the scope and scale of value-added support such as educational programs and marketing materials should also be worked out in advance.

Even if you're part of a larger financial services organization, you can still leverage the relationships the firm has with its suppliers. For instance, if you're working at a brokerage firm, that firm will have agreements with asset management companies and those organizations will have an array of support services that you can tap into.

Next, you can ask your fellow advisors for referrals. When weighing any referrals, you should take into account such factors as the extent of their stated expertise and experience; how they keep up with new trends, products, and regulations; how they're perceived by their peers; what kinds of clients they've worked for; and how they get compensated. Your clients can also be a source of referrals, but you should first have a feel for whether or not a client will be happy to help or may instead end up wondering why you can't come up with experts on your own.

In addition, you can attend seminars and conferences and keep an eye on who's writing columns on the hot topics in trade publications (very often the same experts that are working the seminars and conferences). And remember, it's essential to find people who are not only very good at what they do but who are also comfortable being team players. In a business where self-confidence and a big ego are generally plusses, you and your team members have to realize that there are times when each of you in turn may have to be part of the supporting cast, not the star.

I Finding the Right Specialists

Knowing who's in the lineup and even where to find them doesn't mean the right team is easy to assemble, particularly if you work for yourself. According to a study of 81 independent financial advisors that we conducted in 2002, most were able to find specialists, but there were issues when it came to the expertise and integrity of those specialists (Exhibit 5.3). In fact, each advisor should be able to deliver on each of the following:

I Specific expertise

I Integrity

I Personal chemistry

I Teamwork

Now let's take a closer look at these criteria for choosing advisory partners, beginning with expertise. The field of wealth management, which often intersects with complex tax issues, regularly requires the skills of an expert. And an advisor in a given field, asset protection planning, to name just one, should have precise and up-to-date knowledge on his or her subject and also be able to convey that information in a credible and comprehensible way. Such expertise will not come cheap, but in our research, we have repeatedly found that the affluent want the best available advice and are willing to pay for it.

exhibit 5.3	The challenges of putting an Advisory Team Together

RATED ON A SCALE OF 1 TO 10 WHERE 1 IS EASY AND
10 IS EXTREMELY DIFFICULT

▌ Finding experts with integrity 8.2

▌ Finding technical expertise.........................7.5

▌ Finding experts to work with.......................4.3

n= 81 independent financial advisors. source: Prince & Associates, 2002.

The value of expertise is not just a matter of what a professional knows or even what he or she can convey to the client; that expertise also extends to the information and insights that will rub off to your advantage. Partnering with a leading expert can open a window into the latest industry thinking, an array of risk scenarios, various compensation structures, and new marketing ideas.

▎ The Highest Ethical and Professional Standards

Anyone you partner with should also observe the highest ethical standards whether they're working with you, one another, or your client. Again, the nature of wealth management – and the rewards – can entice some individuals to push up against legal and ethical boundaries, creating anxiety, compromising everyone involved, and possibly sabotaging your relationship with your clients. It's your job to make sure that doesn't happen.

Further, as it's impossible to foresee all of the business opportunities that might come up and negotiate in advance how they'll be remunerated, advisors must not only trust one another, but also be able to articulate and comfortably discuss their ethical standards.

In addition, each advisor in your network should be highly professional in every way, whether it's a matter of promptly returning
phone calls, showing up for meetings on time, or dressing appropriately when seeing one of your clients.

To that end, every specialist to whom you look for expertise, who's
part of your professional network, and who might end up in front
of your clients, must be thoroughly vetted. You can do this a number
of different ways including checking their credentials with other
advisors and conducting formal background checks. You should
also examine their clientele and see how they get new business.

Remember, when you bring an expert on board and introduce him
or her to your client, it's your business and your client relationship that's on the line, not theirs. Failing to cover every angle and
ask every question up front can result in headaches – or worse –
later on.

❙ The question of chemistry

All of the expertise in the world isn't going to be worth much if
there's no rapport between you and the specialist wielding the
knowledge. There needs to be some chemistry between you and
each of the advisors you work with, as well as among the various
specialists – and that job is in your hands, not theirs. When we
asked independent financial advisors about their biggest
challenge when working with other advisors, over one-third cited
a lack of chemistry (Exhibit 5.4). Over three-quarters found that
the experts were not as expert as they professed to be, and nine out
of ten said the specialists they brought in tried to steal their client.

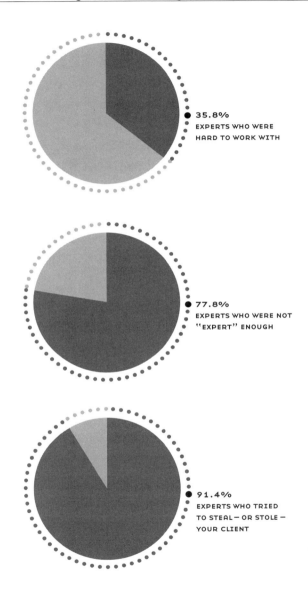

| exhibit 5.4 | The challenges of Advisory Relationships |

35.8%
EXPERTS WHO WERE
HARD TO WORK WITH

77.8%
EXPERTS WHO WERE NOT
"EXPERT" ENOUGH

91.4%
EXPERTS WHO TRIED
TO STEAL — OR STOLE —
YOUR CLIENT

n = 81 Independent Financial Advisors.
Source: Prince & Associates, 2002.

The best way to see if you're going to hit it off is to spend some time together talking about your approach to business or perhaps working on a real life client situation in a strategic scenario session where you brainstorm viable solutions to actual client issues. Choose the test client wisely, however. Addressing the highly complex issues of your most difficult clients may not be much of a proving ground. Instead, choose an "average" client and aim for an issue that requires the advisor's specific knowledge to see how the two of you might work together on the client's behalf.

As for vetting their expertise, there are three moments of truth. First, the original selection process where conversations, referrals, and a sample strategic scenario session should reveal their breadth of knowledge and ability to wield it. Second, when you work together and see how other specialists respond to the suggestions, particularly if there's a specialist from the same field of expertise, such as as another lawyer. And thirdly, any word from the grapevine about what your specialist is doing with other clients and advisors.

｜ Team players wanted

For a network to run smoothly, each advisor has to understand his or her role and to know that it's you who's in charge, you who "owns" the client and know what's best for them. All too often an assembly of high-powered professionals can lead to conflict as egos get rubbed raw, especially when there's only one team leader.

Such turf wars must be avoided because they'll fracture your network and compromise the quality of your client service. Sometimes the fault lies with the wealth manager who fails to set the groundrules for the collaborative process (and forgets what it's like to be part of another advisor's network). At other times, the specialist may commit the cardinal sin of trying to cut the wealth manager out of the loop by working directly with the client. This can be avoided by spelling out your role and theirs upfront, and, most importantly, making it clear that you're in charge. As such, you should be overseeing all client contact. You should also create clear agreements (oral if not written) covering what's presented to the client, as well as when and how it's presented.

ı caution: Advisors Already on Board

For all of the top-tier resources you may be able to muster, many affluent clients will already have a trusted accountant or insurance agent in place and will not be receptive to the idea of their expert being shunted aside. That doesn't mean that you shouldn't have those resources lined up, however, as not every client will have every type of advisor on board.

By using the Whole Client Model, you'll have found out which other advisors your client is using as well as the nature of the relationship. That information will help you when it comes to deciding whether or not to bring in an expert and, if you choose to do so, how best to make it happen. Even if they're completely committed or satisfied with the experts they have, wealthy clients may be open to the idea of a new face and new ideas. In addition, your specialist's particular area of expertise may be of value even if there's some overlap; given the breadth of legal scholarship, one lawyer can certainly inform another on certain aspects of the law.

If your client does have advisors with whom he or she already has a good working relationship, you'll have to be able to make them part of your team with respect to that client. Doing so, however, has its own rewards in that it may lead to referrals. Along the way, you may also have to give up the lead in some cases and act as a team member. In any event, you should at all times avoid being seen an interloper trying to wrest a client away.

| How to pay them

Those wealth managers who have in-house resources to draw upon usually don't have to worry about paying their specialists because they're part of the financial institution's advisor support system. Some wealth managers, whether independent or part of a larger firm, set up formal teams where the specialists are part of their own boutique operation. And other wealth managers establish a "virtual boutique."

In general, however, there are two principal ways to compensate the experts who are part of your professional network. The first is to put them on retainer (although some advisors such as attorneys may prefer hourly rates), a situation where the wealth manager is taking the economic risk.

The other way to compensate the specialists is on a variable or contingency basis, giving the expert a portion of the revenue. For example, you might have a life insurance expert as part of your professional network, and when a life insurance sale is made, you split the commission. In this case, the specialist is shouldering the economic burden and, not surprisingly, it's more cost-effective and less risky for you as the wealth manager.

| staying state of the art

Over the last few years, there's been a steady stream of new financial products, services, and tools designed specifically, and in many cases exclusively, for affluent clients. At the same time, legislation and regulations that, depending on who's in the White House, either extend or proscribe the financial rights of the wealthy are regularly being introduced or revised. In short, there's a lot to keep up with out there. But keep up you must because, in the same way they want the newest technology, the affluent also want to be sure they have access to whatever's hot in the world of wealth management. Recall the recent feeding frenzy over hedge funds. The affluent want to take advantage of the financial perks that are emblematic of their wealth.

For wealth managers, that means keeping tabs on the latest and greatest products. Some cutting-edge ideas result in a new sale; all of them should enable you to better serve your affluent clients. And staying state of the art is a key point of differentiation in the world of wealth management, so you should always know which ideas are fresh out of the box, even if you put them back unused.

It's not just new products and services, of course, but also the latest strategies and tactics used to manage affluence. Wealth managers have to keep up with the evolving legal and regulatory landscape. They have to know how the tax laws change in various jurisdictions, what effect the changes might have on the affluent, and which tax court cases, IRS memoranda, regulations, and private letter rulings need to be considered.

So how do you find the cutting edge? Once upon a time, industry conferences and seminars were the prime hunting ground. But the top innovators more jealously guard their ideas these days. A number of trade publications have become barren for the same reason. As a result, your best bet is the professional relationships you've established with industry experts – your advisory team members and the other authorities that you're acquainted with.

Given that framework, the best forums for staying state of the art are the strategic scenario sessions that you conduct with your team. In the course of considering a client's unique situation and brainstorming ideas and solutions, you (and the rest of your team) will all benefit from one another's up-to-date expertise and learn by seeing how that expertise can be applied to specific client situations. In sum, if you make sure that the members of your team are well-informed and easy to partner with, you'll benefit from your interactions with them on many levels.

A chain Reaction of Expertise

In many cases, the act of lining up an expert resource can set off a chain reaction of introductions to, and relationships with, other specialists. Consider the case of Ruth, an independent financial advisor adept at investment management. When expanding into wealth management, she set about building the advisory team that would complement her expertise. She started with the trusts and estates lawyer who worked for one of her wealthier clients. In partnering with the lawyer, she found him easy to work with and realized that he was recognized by his peers as a leading authority in the field. The lawyer, in turn, introduced her to a life insurance expert who specialized in using life insurance as an estate planning tool. After informing the lawyer that many of her clients were senior corporate executives, he also introduced her to a derivatives specialist who could adroitly manage concentrated stock positions, and the derivatives specialist knew a leading securities lawyer who could be brought in as needed. The trusts and estates lawyer also introduced her to an accountant who was capable of providing income tax strategies and planning as well as valuation services. In the end, by meeting one advisor through a common client, Ruth was able to put together the core components of her advisory network.

self-diagnostic

▎ evaluating your technical competencies

Before assembling your advisory resources, it's important to get a better idea of what you do - and don't - know about the three component parts of wealth management: brokerage, investment management, and advanced planning.

On page 95, we provided a checklist of the basic wealth management products, services, and strategies. In the following exercise, we'll provide examples of how you should assess your competence for a specific element of each wealth management component. Keep in mind that you can conduct similar exercises for all of the items on page 95 (and others) as they come up in your practice and then decide how much expertise you need to tap into.

Using the scale below, rate how adept you are at each of the following:

not at all competent   *extremely competent*

< 1   2   3   4   5   6   7   8   9   10 >

▎ In considering **brokerage**, let's look at managing a concentrated stock position as an example.

▎ PURCHASE OF PUTS

▎ ZERO PREMIUM COLLARS

▎ PUT SPREAD COLLARS

▎ MONETIZED COLLARS

▎ VARIABLE PRE-PAID FORWARDS

▎ 90% NON-RECOURSE LOANS

If your score for any of the above is less than **7**, you need to learn more or bring in a specialist.

▮ Now let's focus on an element of **investment management**,
portfolio construction and maintenance. For each of the following
components of portfolio management, rate your competency
using the same scale:

▮ PORTFOLIO CONSTRUCTION   ☐

▮ BENCHMARKING   ☐

▮ SECURITY SELECTION   ☐

▮ ASSET ALLOCATION   ☐

▮ SECTOR WEIGHTING   ☐

▮ PERFORMANCE ATTRIBUTION   ☐

▮ RISK DISPERSION   ☐

▮ PORTFOLIO POSITIONING   ☐

Again, a score of **7** or less for any discipline means you'll either
need to become more expert in the area or have to outsource the
function. Remember that there are a lot of top financial advisors
who readily recognize their lack of expertise in these areas. Instead
of doing money management themselves, for instance, they use
packaged products such as mutual funds and managed accounts to
provide discretionary portfolio management.

continued

| Finally, let's examine more closely a specific area of
advanced planning, charitable giving:

- **OUTRIGHT GIFTS** ☐
- **CHARITABLE BEQUESTS** ☐
- **LIFE INSURANCE** ☐
- **GIFT ANNUITIES** ☐
- **POOLED INCOME FUNDS** ☐
- **CHARITABLE REMAINDER TRUSTS** ☐
- **CHARITABLE LEAD TRUSTS** ☐
- **DONOR-ADVISED FUNDS** ☐
- **SUPPORTING ORGANIZATIONS** ☐
- **PRIVATE FOUNDATIONS** ☐

A score of less than **7** for any of the above is a signal that you must either enhance your knowledge concerning this type of charitable giving product/strategy or bring in the requisite expertise.

the wealth management team

| THE THREE WEALTH MANAGEMENT TEAM STRUCTURES

| THE STRUCTURES, PRO AND CON

| FINDING COMMON GROUND AND COMMON GOALS

| DON'T FORGET THE FEEDBACK

For financial advisors who hope to become wealth managers, the most daunting step may be establishing and running a professional network. Many advisors are accustomed to operating on their own and having a targeted – and limited – client focus. Bringing the right resources together and playing nicely with other advisors is simply not part of their job description or experience. As a wealth manager, however, you'll be enmeshed in, and dependent on, a network of specialists. And to be successful, you'll have to know how to get the most out of them and keep everyone happy along the way.

Wealth managers who have put together effective professional networks have discovered that they must find the time and resources to learn how to become facilitators. Being a team leader is not something that anyone can easily add to their resume, but it's nonetheless a commitment that needs to be made.

In the preceding chapter, we addressed a number of issues surrounding the creation of the wealth management team. We looked at the role of the team, where you can find the right specialists, what to do when a client already has specialists on the payroll, and how to compensate specialists.

In this chapter, we'll take a closer look at the three main wealth management team structures and consider what they can mean for you and the way you do business.

▮ wealth management team structures

Depending on your particular situation, whether you are, for instance, part of a large firm or work for yourself, there are three wealth management team structures:

exhibit 6.1 The parent company as team

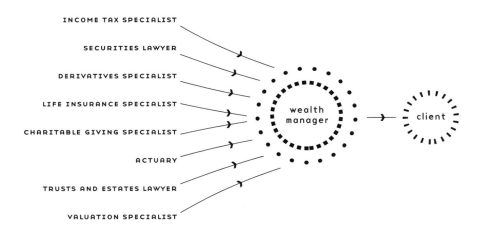

Conceptually, this is the most straightforward organizational structure, whereby all of the various experts you might require are employed by the financial institution where you work and are available to you on an as-needed basis.

exhibit 6.2 | The self-contained team

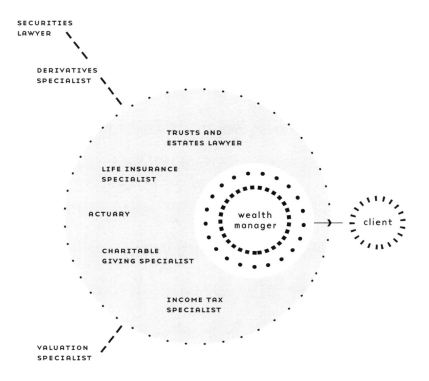

In this case, a number of the specialists whose expertise you need on a regular basis are formally part of your core organization and "employed" by you. They are usually paid a salary and a bonus based on the profitability of the entire team and their individual contribution to that profitability as measured by you, the team leader. Because some other experts are less frequently required, they wouldn't be part of the core team but would be available on an as-needed basis.

exhibit 6.3	The virtual team

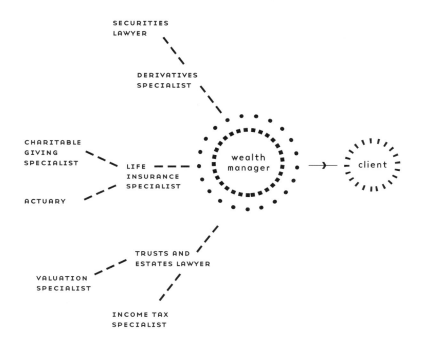

As the leader of a Virtual Team, you would work alone and bring in specialists when you need them. It's not uncommon for you to have well-defined relationships with three experts – a life insurance specialist, a trusts and estates lawyer, and a derivatives specialist – each of whom would have, in turn, specialists who they work with and manage.

These three wealth management team structures should be thought of as hypothetical. In practice, the differences are subtle and there's often considerable overlap. The Self-Contained Team structure, for example, has a number of virtual elements. In some larger financial institutions, the Parent Company as Team can often be combined with the Self-Contained Team. Your wealth management team roster will vary depending on your business model, your clientele, your current affiliations, and your finances. However, to better define the three structures hypothetically, we'll use the following team roster:

I The wealth manager whose technical specialty is brokerage and/or investment management;

I The derivatives specialist responsible for dealing with concentrated stock positions;

I The securities lawyer who supports the derivatives specialist;

I The life insurance specialist;

I The actuary who's often needed when dealing with certain life insurance issues;

I The attorney whose expertise is in charitable giving;

I The trusts and estates lawyer;

I The income tax authority (i.e., an accountant); and

I The valuation expert who would be called in to appraise business interests, real estate, or collectibles.

I Some Pros and Cons

Of course, each of the wealth management team structures has its advantages and drawbacks (Exhibit 6.4). The cost of maintaining a Self-Contained Team, for example, can be high compared to the other structures, but it can be justified when there's enough business. For the Parent Company as Team, the financial institution bears the cost and it's economical by virtue of being distributed over many advisors. With the Virtual Team, presuming the expertise is paid for when used, the cost is variable.

For the Self-Contained Team, you (and your clients) can get help in a hurry whereas, for the Parent Company as Team and the Virtual Team, the experts could be busy and unable to respond to your requests as promptly as you might hope.

When it comes to industry trends and knowledge, the Parent Company as Team is generally able to stay state-of-the-art because of its resources and people. The Virtual Team can also stay up-to-date because of the specialists selected and the need of these specialists to maintain their position as leading authorities. Often, they are aware of, or even involved in, innovations. It's somewhat more difficult for experts on the Self-Contained Team to stay at the cutting edge due to their often constant need to apply their knowledge and talents to client situations, sometimes to the exclusion of other activities such as training and research.

As your wealth management practice evolves, you'll often see the need to drop some experts and bring others aboard. This is most easily accomplished in the Parent Company as Team structure because everyone will be in the firm somewhere and there's no stigma or diplomacy required to add and subtract experts. It's somewhat harder in the Virtual Team structure as disengaging existing professional relationships and establishing new ones can be problematic. It's most difficult of all to change the roster of the Self-Contained Team because they're employees or have a more formalized relationship with you. If you do let them go, either because they're not up to the job or because it turns out to be an expertise you don't need as often as you thought, be sure they've signed a non-compete contract so that they don't go after your clients (such contracts are usually signed when you hire them).

exhibit 6.4	comparing the wealth management team structures		
ISSUE	THE PARENT COMPANY AS TEAM	THE SELF-CONTAINED TEAM	THE VIRTUAL TEAM
Cost of maintaining the wealth management team	Low	High	Low
Accessibility and responsiveness	Medium	High	Medium
Ability to stay state-of-the-art	High	Medium	High
The challenge of adding or subtracting team members	Low	High	Medium

ı establishing a common vision and goals

No matter which structure is right for you, when building a team you'll also have to meet with prospective team members to hammer out your shared goals and vision. Some of the issues where consensus is crucial include:

ı Whose client is it?

ı Why these specialists (and disciplines)?

ı How will all involved parties communicate?

ı How are ideas going to be presented to the client?

ı Under what conditions are specialists going to be placed in front of the client?

Some of these issues are especially challenging in a financial services culture that's built around the "hand-off"—where clients are usually passed from one expert to another for specialized solutions, an approach antithetical to the idea of wealth management. But they must be addressed if the wealth management model is to work.

In some instances, formal team development training is used to help a team come together. The training can involve experiential exercises where team members come to understand the benefits of relying on others and see how a group is able to achieve what individuals cannot.

Building cohesiveness is not a one-time event, however. You'll have to regenerate this feeling over and over again. In the fast-paced world of advisory services, it's easy to fall back into old patterns of thinking. So you'll have to be constantly aware of how members of your team are doing, and be imaginative in devising ways for them to recommit to their shared goal of comprehensive and client-centered wealth management. One effective way to promote teamwork is by involving all of your specialists in strategic scenario sessions, even though their field of expertise may not be needed in a given session, because it reinforces their importance to the overall team.

Keep in mind that, as the leader, you have certain advantages. First, most advisors will see that, within the context of wealth management, the team can get more business than they can get on their own. Further, you're the one that put the team together, after all, and the professionals on board will have already been vetted to some degree by their firm, clients, or other experts who referred them, or by you (and they will have likewise examined you and your business prospects to see if it's worth their while to work with you). That means that you'll have talked to them and their references, know that they're capable of being team players, and have established at least a working level of professional respect and trust beforehand. That spade work should make it that much easier to keep the group together and contributing.

We've found that the best way to keep your team motivated is by succeeding. And the more you succeed the happier and more motivated – and wealthier – your team members will be. Therefore, by doing business in volume, you're going to keep your teammates interested and committed.

ı The Binding Power of Feedback

No matter what steps you take, some members of your advisory network may not have the time or inclination to engage in the more touchy-feely approach to team building – and that's not necessarily a strike against them. If they're so inclined, the best way to create cohesiveness is by conducting the strategic scenario sessions that we've already referred to, during which members of the team brainstorm actual wealth management solutions based on an affluent client's specific financial situation. The issue on the table could involve a complicated business succession plan, a messy second marriage, dissolving a trust, or realigning a bond-heavy portfolio. No matter what the scenario, the act of bringing the team's combined knowledge to bear on the subject – and the respect shown for each advisor's expertise – will be binding when you convert these ideas into better serving the client and generating revenues.

During these sessions, it's essential that there should be no constraints or time limits on feedback. The specialists should be encouraged to offer an opinion and share an idea, even if it's still germinating. This is where your facilitative skills will come in handy. Constantly seeking feedback sets an important precedent for the give-and-take between experts and it's also a sign of respect – you're making it clear to your team members that you want to know what they think. As anyone who's ever been on the receiving end can tell you, positive feedback from fellow professionals works wonders. And if you keep rewarding great teamwork with public affirmation, you'll be communicating and reinforcing your goals at the same time.

case study

The Team at Work

Gerald, a wealth manager, found that by including all of the specialists on his team in each strategic scenario sessions he was able to accomplish a number of goals. First, by walking through the answers the client had provided to the Whole Client Model, the team identified unexpected opportunities to provide additional services and products. Further, in working together, they were able to better recognize the value of each team member, thereby building solidarity and strengthening the team.

ı centering the Advisory Team

You and the members of your advisory team will all benefit by keeping everyone on the same page at all times. We've found the following exercise can be useful in that regard. Note: This exercise can be conducted face to face or over the phone.

ı **WHAT HAVE WE BEEN TRYING TO ACCOMPLISH?**

ı **WHAT HAVE WE BEEN DOING THAT WORKS WELL?**

ı **WHAT HAVE WE BEEN DOING THAT HASN'T WORKED WELL?**

ı **WHAT OPPORTUNITIES ARE WE MISSING?**

ı **WHICH WEALTH MANAGEMENT PRODUCT OR SERVICE DO WE WANT TO USE NEXT?**

ı **WHAT ARE WE GOING TO DO TO MOVE THE PRACTICE FORWARD?**

Think of this exercise in the way that NFL coaches might act after a game, whether the team won or lost: They would sit down and watch the game films, evaluate the performance, and get ready for the next game with the intent of doing much better.

Keep in mind that there are no right or wrong answers to these questions. They're intended to help everyone involved understand where the practice has been successful and where it may have hit a speed bump or two. The questions are also helpful when it comes to getting everyone on the team involved and looking ahead.

What have we been trying to accomplish? This gives you the opportunity to survey the members of your advisory team, to better understand their business perspectives, and to see if there's any dissension or confusion among the specialists. You can reaffirm the benefits of wealth management and reinforce how it's not only the model that affluent clients want, but it's potentially more profitable for everyone on the team. In the process, you can also redirect your collective efforts in any new direction and, most importantly, build a unified vision for the team.

What have we been doing that works well? By asking this question, you'll be able to get a clear understanding of what's working well for both the client and the specialist. It also gives you the chance to reaffirm how well the specialists have been performing and how much energy they've been expending on behalf of the team.

What have we been doing that hasn't worked well? A more complicated prospect, this will allow you to address, and hopefully fix, any glitches that may have come up along the way. For your part, it's vital not to be accusing — good or bad, what's been accomplished should be seen in the context of the team as a whole. It will also give you the chance to see how the specialists react and respond to criticism: Will they bite back or will they learn from their mistakes and try to do better next time?

What opportunities are we missing? In the course of working with clients and one another, the team members should regularly be discovering new ways to package their individual or collective services. This, after all, is one of the key premises that drives wealth management: The more you know about your clients, the more products and services you can deliver to them in a holistic way. As the partnership evolves, new ways of introducing the specialists and their services should regularly present themselves.

Which wealth management product or service do we want to use next? A follow-up to the previous question, this will help you see which specific products and services might be appropriate for individual clients based on the client/specialist interactions to date.

What are we going to do to move the practice forward? No matter how successful the team may be, there will always be the opportunity to improve. Forward progress may be a matter of entering into alliances or more formal arrangements with accountants or attorneys, or it may involve understanding and integrating the latest and greatest wealth management products and services that the team specialists may be aware of before they hit the mainstream (the latter being one of the main reasons for having the specialists on hand in the first place). In either case, forward-thinking and forward-planning will also build team spirit and solidarity.

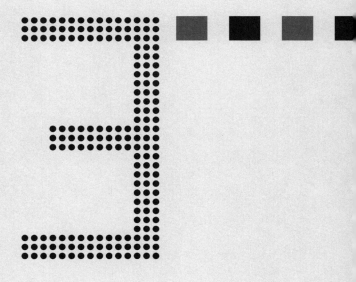

grading, keeping, and transitioning your clients

- WHAT IS WEALTH MANAGEMENT?
- WHEN IT COMES TO CLIENTS, THINK QUALITY NOT QUANTITY
- CALCULATE THE VALUE OF YOUR CURRENT CLIENTS
- RETROFIT CLIENTS SO THAT THEY UNDERSTAND YOUR NEW ROLE AS A WEALTH MANAGER
- CONDUCT STRATEGIC SCENARIO SESSIONS
- TRANSITION YOUR LESS-PROFITABLE CLIENTS TO OTHER ADVISORS

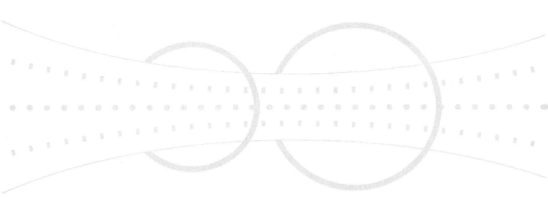

when you become a wealth manager, your client roster is probably going to change – sometimes dramatically. The guiding premise of wealth management is that you can make your business more profitable by offering each affluent client a wider range of products and services in a consultative way. But some of your current clients will not be good candidates for those expanded services, especially over the long term, and they need to be transitioned to other advisors (Exhibit 7.1).

exhibit 7.1	Transitioning clients

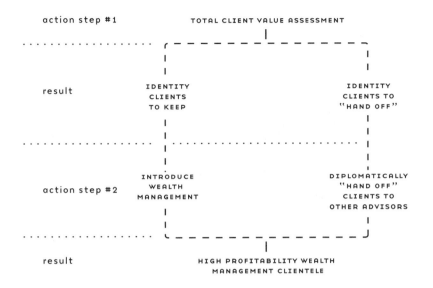

You need to start by assessing the potential that exists in your client base, that is, determine the total value of each client. We've found that such an approach in the context of wealth management gives you a different perspective on your clients and you can readily identify the ones you do and don't want to serve. The former need to be educated and informed about your evolved business model, wealth management, while the less profitable clients need to be diplomatically transitioned to other advisors. (The important next step, finding new clients, will be addressed in the next chapter.)

ı where the profits come from

We should underscore the importance of having a small stable of affluent clients who want wealth management rather than too many clients – especially too many less-affluent clients – who can only divert your time and eat into your profitability.

This conclusion is supported by studies we conducted in 2000 and 2001 during which we asked 177 financial planners and 72 RIAs to take a close look at their businesses and see where they made their money. As the exhibit below illustrates, 80% of those revenues came from about a one-third of their clients. Read the other way, about 70% of the clients accounted for just 20% of total revenues (Exhibit 7.2).

exhibit 7.2	client profitability	
PERCENTAGE OF CLIENTS ACCOUNTING FOR 80% OF REVENUES		
	2000	2001
Financial Planners	30.3%	27.6%
RIAs	38.7%	31.4%

n = 249 financial planners and RIAs
source: Prince & Associates, 2000 and 2001

Clearly, not every client warrants equal time and attention. Further, as previously noted, we've conducted a number of studies over the past few years on both the client and advisor side that have corroborated another truism: The more quality time you spend with affluent clients, the more production you can expect. It's also worth remembering that most affluent clients have more than one advisor these days, so each advisor is being measured against the others, and the opportunity to win more assets, cross-sell, and get referrals depends on the quality and intensity of the relationship. That relationship, in turn, hinges on how much quality time is put against it.

Combining that need for quality time with the above statistics leads us to a conclusion most advisors already implicitly understand: they have too many clients and not enough time to attend to them all. Indeed, the top performers in the financial services industry are those who have done the best job of interacting with clients, especially affluent clients. Often, that means paring your client roster and delegating administrative work so that you can get more face-time with your wealthiest clients.

No surprises so far. But it's the next steps that are the high hurdles for advisors transitioning to wealth management. We all realize that the plum clients are the ones with enough assets to generate income even if those clients don't do much with those assets. The bigger issues are how to decide which other clients have the most potential – which clients are the best ones to spend time with – and, by inference, which ones should be dropped.

₁ Total client value

One of the most popular ways to rank clients is the A-B-C system where "A" clients are the ones with the most assets under management and "C's" are the ones with the fewest assets. That's fine for maintaining the status quo, but it won't help you figure out which clients hiding among the "B's" and "C's" are the ones with the greatest wealth management profit potential – which ones might be the source of more assets to manage, more cross-selling opportunities, and more referrals.

There's no foolproof system for measuring profit potential, of course, but we can get a close enough estimate to rank current clients by entering numbers into the following Total Client Value formula:

TOTAL CLIENT VALUE   =   CURRENT AUM
+
OTHER INVESTABLE ASSETS
+
CROSS-SELLING OPPORTUNITIES
+
FUTURE REFERRALS

ı what else Do They Have?

Breaking the formula down, current AUM, or assets under management, is the money you're already managing on their behalf, a figure that you'll generally have on hand so it's easy to plug in. When it comes to additional investable assets – bank accounts, accounts with other advisors, an inheritance on the way – it's going to call for some feel and finesse. Many advisors may have a close enough relationship to go ahead and ask a client outright about their other investable assets. The Whole Client Model, detailed on pages 77-80, is another way to educe the information you're looking for. In still other cases, it may be a matter of piecework or of falling back on your business instincts and professional judgement. (It's worth noting that those clients most likely to share information about their assets may also be the best prospects for wealth management because an open and high-quality relationship already exists.)

Aside from investable assets, the Whole Client Model uncovers the other assets that are not investable such as business interests, land, and collectibles. If you were merely providing investment type services, these assets wouldn't be relevant. But, as a wealth manager, these assets are the point and the opportunity because use of the wealth management model often converts them into investable assets.

ı what else Do They want?

In the process of uncovering other assets, you'll often get a better idea of which wealth management opportunities to focus on. In talking to a client, you may find that he or she has, for instance, an outdated estate plan, unfulfilled charitable intentions, a bloated money market fund, or a daughter thinking of going back to medical school. That knowledge could in turn lead to, respectively, a new life insurance policy, a donor-advised fund, a managed account, or a 529 plan. Other opportunities can be added to the equation based on what you already know about the client. If the client is a business owner, there's key person life insurance and various funding options for buy/sell agreements. If she's newly remarried, she may want to review and rewrite her will. And when the recommended product or service is not one where you're an expert, the time will be right to bring in one of the specialists on your wealth management team.

What else do they need?

Clients and prospects are rarely familiar with all the financial services and products available to them. Often they only have a rough idea of what they want to accomplish financially (that's where you come in), let alone which tools will help them get there.

As we have seen, the consultative nature of the wealth management model enables you to help affluent clients better understand their needs and wants and, as such, set their financial agenda. The broad array of wealth management services and products can then be brought to the table. Further, by understanding what your wealthy clients want and need, you're opening the door to a variety of cross-selling opportunities. For example, let's say that by using the Whole Client Model you find that a client is concerned about establishing a charitable legacy but wants to equitably divide her estate between her two children, one of whom has been groomed to take over the family business. The client also wants to keep the family together, particularly her grandchildren, three from one child and two from the other. With this knowledge in hand, you can create an estate plan that leaves one child the family business outright, using life insurance to pay the estate taxes on the business. Her other child will be given the responsibility of managing a newly-created family foundation that has been initially funded with $3 million that you'll manage. The grandchildren, meanwhile, would stay in touch because they would be involved in the foundation's grant-making process. Finally, a second life insurance policy for your client could be used to leave something to the child who was not left the family business.

ı who else do they know?

When gauging the number of potential referrals, it's going to once more be a matter of common sense and informed guesswork rather than hard science. In fact, you might have to use a ballpark figure extrapolated from their business and social status rather than an actual list of names. Referrals have to be earned, of course, but by devoting more time and a wealth management mindset to those clients with the greatest total value, the odds of getting referrals may well improve. Consider, for instance, a client who owns a mid-sized manufacturing company. When calculating the referral opportunities, you can include his fellow business owners, particularly those who live locally, his clients, and his vendors.

ı Grading Your clientele using the Total client value Formula: A case study

To see how the Total Client Value formula works, let's look at the experience of a financial advisor who subsequently moved to the wealth management model. As an advisor, he categorized his clients using the A-B-C approach; as a wealth manager he moved to the Total Client Value formula, and, as a result, the scope of his client assessment capability changed dramatically (Exhibit 7.3).

| The "A" clients:

client #1: Jim, 73, is a retired executive with $1,400,000 in a discretionary investment account which was rolled over into an IRA. He doesn't have any other meaningful assets and, having recently moved, he has lost touch with his former colleagues. His advisor bought and sold securities in this account generating, on average, 60 basis points a year for an annual revenue from this client of $8,400.

Because there were no other assets and Jim didn't know anyone else with money, the opportunity to provide additional financial services and products was limited and there probably wouldn't be any referrals. Consequently, using the Total Client Value approach, Jim's value remained at $8,400.

client #2: Sean is a 58-year-old senior executive at a large, publicly-traded manufacturing company. He had $800,000 in a discretionary account with his advisor that generated about $8,000 a year in fees.

Sean also had $21,000,000 in low-basis stock, the kind of non-investable asset that a wealth manager can work with. By hedging this position, with a fee of 25 basis points, the advisor generated an additional $52,500 in fees. Sean then took a loan against the position and thus had $16,800,000 to invest. At one percent a year, that added up to $168,000 annually.

Further, Sean knew a number of other executives at his company with concentrated stock positions who were also looking to diversify. Two of them had $22,000,000 in near zero-basis company stock and no other assets. By hedging these positions, at a fee of 25 basis points, the advisor earned $55,000. By taking a loan against those positions, the advisor could potentially have another $17,600,000 to invest or another $176,000 in income.

ı The "B" clients:

client #3: Shelli is a small business owner with $250,000 in a managed account from which her advisor had an annual income of $2,500.

She had another $300,000 in a savings account, half of which could be moved to the managed account, resulting in additional fees of $1,500 annually. Shelli didn't have – but needed – key person insurance, which would result in a commission of $40,000. She also knew other small business owners in the area who she thought to be good candidates for key person life insurance or other planning services and was willing to refer them. Her advisor anticipated at least one life insurance sale based on a referral for a projected commission of $20,000, bringing Shelli's Total Client Value to $64,000.

client #4: Matt is a family business owner with a $650,000 stock portfolio producing an average of $5,000 a year in revenue for the advisor who had done no financial, estate, or tax planning whatsoever.

The cost of an estate plan was $1,300 and the commission on life insurance was $20,000 (the life insurance had been purchased to pay estate taxes).

There were also three family members with combined investable assets of $840,000 and the advisor could assume control of those accounts. All told, the total value of this client was $36,200.

▮ The "c" clients:

client #5: Marissa is a working artist who had a SEP IRA worth $200,000 that generated $2,000 in fees annually. Though there weren't any cross-sell opportunities with this client, she was well known and had a number of affluent friends and clients. Using the Whole Client Model, the advisor was able to put together a long list of possible referrals which could be worth as much as $40,000 a year in additional revenue for investment management services in the first year.

client #6: Claire is a teacher with $40,000 in mutual funds that produced $320 in annual fees. Through referrals to five other teachers, her advisor could potentially pick up another $50,000 to manage. These additional assets would result in another $400 annually, putting the total value of this client at $720.

exhibit 7.3	using the Total Client Value Approach				
CLIENT	CURRENT FEES/INCOME	ADDITIONAL FEES/INCOME	ADDITIONAL SERVICES-PRODUCTS	REFERRALS (QUANTIFIED)	TOTAL
CLIENT #1	$8,400	—	—	—	$8,400
CLIENT #2	$8,000	$168,000	$52,500	$231,000	$459,500
CLIENT #3	$2,500	$1,500	$40,000	$20,000	$64,000
CLIENT #4	$5,000	—	$21,300	$9,900	$36,200
CLIENT #5	$2,000	—	—	$40,000	$42,000
CLIENT #6	$320	—	—	$400	$720

Current revenue = $26,220

Total potential revenues as a wealth manager = $610,820

By using the Total Client Value formula, the advisor was able to prioritize his clients and increase his revenues by concentrating on Clients 2, 3, and 5. Client 4 still had some potential and might be worth working with depending on the time involved, but Client 1 and 6 would be better off with another advisor who would give them the time and attention they deserve.

ı Retrofitting Existing Clients

One complication is the fact that your current clients aren't necessarily going to accept that you've gone from being their financial advisor to a wealth manager who deserves more of their trust and business just because you say so. Even those clients with whom you have a great relationship may require an explanation of how you became a wealth manager and what that means for them.

The first step is to do your homework. Being able to persuade clients that you're a wealth manager, particularly those clients who've known you as a financial advisor, will be your proving ground, and you're going to have to prepare for them a presentation that will win them over. That presentation should be from the client's perspective, that is, not about what's in it for you, but how they'll benefit from a more consultative relationship and the chance to get the full menu of products and services from a single source. You should address the fact that many affluent clients are looking for a personal CFO to help them manage their wealth. You should give them examples of clients who you have worked with and what you've done for them. Lastly, you should emphasize that wealth managers are there to solve problems, not sell products, a point that will surely resonate with any client, affluent or otherwise.

That should cover why you became a wealth manager; now you have to move on to how you became one. You should define for your clients what wealth management is, what it entails, and why you're qualified. Then tell them, for instance, about the professional network that you've assembled and how you can coordinate the various experts on their behalf.

ı strategic scenario sessions

As part of this process, you often need to come in armed with specific financial ideas that go beyond what you were previously providing to your client, ideas that will also help validate you as a wealth manager in their eyes. To do this, you can turn to your professional network and conduct the strategic scenario sessions that we have already referred to, reviewing with your specialists what you know about the affluent client and then brainstorming viable financial strategies and solutions.

There are a number of different ways to run strategic scenario sessions and they all hinge on your understanding of the client (which brings us back to the Whole Client Model). As noted, strategic scenario sessions are brainstorming meetings where you and your team think through a client's financial situation and then identify applicable solutions. Such sessions are only successful to the extent that there's not only a systematic way to share information and come up with ideas, but also an efficient method for capturing any insights and translating them into a viable action plan.

When you begin to make presentations, start with those clients with whom you have a strong working relationship because they'll give you honest feedback and be most likely to accept the transition of your business model to wealth management. Fine-tune your presentation and then move on to clients for whom you've been able to come up with financial solutions based on the strategic scenario sessions. Then, when the presentation has been further tweaked, deliver it to those clients who you've determined to have the higher Total Client Value, partly because they're the greatest source of potential profit but also because they're probably the best candidates for wealth management.

ı placing Your Former clients

Even while you're busy trying to persuade your high-value clients that you can do more as a wealth manager than you could as a financial advisor, you're going to have to begin to take the next, and hardest step: transitioning those clients whose Total Client Value doesn't warrant your full attention. To do that, you'll first need to think about how many clients you can profitably manage. The magic number will vary dramatically from wealth manager to wealth manager based on the business model, income goals, and such resources as fellow advisors and business or client administrators. Some wealth managers may want to be the only one who ever talks with their top clients while others may be comfortable handing off that job on occasion. Whatever the number may be, it's a safe bet that every wealth manager will have some less-profitable clients who must be transitioned.

Those with the most assets obviously stay – with a renewed awareness that there may not be much more profit in them. After that, an advisor should keep those clients with the greatest Total Client Value and, to be on the safe side, those who seem to have potential but didn't make the grade because there wasn't enough information to precisely determine their Total Client Value.

Again, as a wealth manager you'll only have the time to effectively manage the client relationship, coordinate the appropriate specialists, and contribute your financial expertise to a relatively short list of affluent clients. If you're going to give those clients what they want, you can't afford to be distracted by the clients who are not worth your time, financially speaking. But you must be responsible for finding other qualified advisors who can give them the time and attention they deserve.

Further, the process of transitioning clients to other advisors is, as a rule, incremental. The more your wealth management practice grows and becomes profitable, the more select and streamlined your client roster will become (especially if you're also attracting new affluent clients). That means your client roster is never static and you must always be prepared to add or subtract clients.

ı ʙe ᴅιrect and ғιnd a ʀeplacement

It's never easy letting a client go, but there are two basic rules: be direct and have a qualified replacement in place. That way, even if there's a raw end to a longstanding client relationship, you'll have made sure not to leave a client hanging. Realistically, you're doing the right thing not only for your own practice but for the client as well since you're not going to be able to devote the necessary time and resources to that client whereas your replacement will. You will also have helped a fellow advisor who may in turn pass along or share an affluent client.

Before you make any move along these lines, create a positioning statement that explains how, because of the types of sophisticated and complex services you now provide, you can't cost effectively (for the client or yourself) be of service. Support your case with examples of the cost of sophisticated wealth management solutions such as funds of funds that require a minimum investment of $5 million.

Next, line up a financial advisor to take over the client. Meet with that advisor and bring him or her up to speed on the client. With a quality advisor ready to take over, talk to the client and create a "halo" for the new advisor, explaining why he or she is a great choice. Then the best approach is for the three of you to meet face-to-face in a meeting that you guide. After the client and advisor have met, you should follow up and have another advisor lined up just in case the new relationship doesn't take.

Keep in mind that clients aren't going to be happy to be dropped and egos will be further bruised when they realize they've been let go because they're not rich enough. Not every ending will be happy, but being upfront is nonetheless the best approach.

Letting Go of Clients

In evaluating his roster of clients, Peter realized that only about 20% of them generated sufficient revenue based on his business model and financial objectives or were good wealth management prospects. That meant he had to transition nearly 100 clients to other advisors. Of that 100, there were about 80 with whom he had limited contact, and they were relatively easy to hand off to the newer advisors in his office. He sat down with each of these advisors and gave them as much detail as he could about each of the clients to ease the transition. He then wrote a letter to each client explaining that the new advisor was available to them and what that advisor's strengths were, after which the advisor contacted the client. The remaining 20 clients that had to be transitioned were far more difficult either because Peter had worked for them since he began in the business or because he had a great working relationship with them. He had to arrange to meet face-to-face with them and brought along a new advisor for them to meet. He explained the types of services he was now providing, such as private placement variable life insurance, hedge funds, and highly sophisticated estate planning techniques. He then explained why the new advisor was an excellent replacement for their needs.

ı Grading your clients

To get an idea of the additional value and revenue that wealth management can uncover in your current client roster, use the grid below to assess the total client value of ten of your better clients. Start by identifying which services and products you're providing today as well as the revenues generated. As a wealth manager, consider what additional pools of investable assets are potentially available as well as those other services and products that you're going to provide. In addition, come up with a ballpark number for the revenues that referrals from this client could produce in a year. Then add up the numbers and rank the clients based on their total client value.

CLIENT	CURRENT AUM	ADDITIONAL INVESTABLE ASSETS	ADDITIONAL SERVICES-PRODUCTS	REFERRALS (QUANTIFIED)	TOTAL

CURRENT REVENUE $ _____

TOTAL POTENTIAL REVENUES AS A WEALTH MANAGER $ _____

establishing new client relationships

I PROSPECTING TOOLS OF THE TRADE

I THE POWER OF REFERRALS

I CLIENTS REFERRALS VS. THOSE FROM CENTERS OF INFLUENCE

I WOMEN AND WEALTH MANAGERS

Regardless of how many clients you keep or transition, there's always room for new and wealthier ones. And as much as we'd like to pass on the secret formula for winning over the rich, there's no such thing. As you'll see in Exercise 8 on page 154, there are a number of ways to get new clients, with referrals solidly in place at the head of the list. Indeed, part of the beauty of wealth management is that it helps you cut a wider swath through the advisory world and creates more opportunities for referrals from the other professionals you interact with as well as from your current clients. Other approaches can include the firm you work with, direct mail, and, the old standard, cold calling. In every case, make sure your wealth management positioning pitch is well honed and ready to be launched. And once you do connect with an affluent prospect, don't let go.

exhibit 8.1	How to find new clients

- Referrals from current clients
- Referrals from accountants
- Referrals from lawyers
- Referrals from other financial advisors
- Referrals from inside the firm where you work
- Seminars
- Public relations/advertising
- Direct mail
- Cold calling

prospecting Tools

There are lots of tried and true ways to prospect (Exhibit 8.1). The real issues are what you get back for the time you invest and what is the quality of the clientele you connect with; in other words, which prospecting tools are going to find the best candidates for wealth management? Based on a series of surveys that we have conducted over the past few years, there are two clear winners: referrals from clients and from centers of influence, the lawyers and accountants who work with the affluent (Exhibit 8.2).

In studies conducted in 1997, 2000, and 2003, we asked hundreds of financial advisors how they had landed their top twenty clients during the preceding two-year period. As noted, referrals from current clients and centers of influence dominated the field to the near exclusion of every other form of prospecting, which never added up to more than 5% of the total. This doesn't invalidate the use of those tools — cold calling can work — but it does pinpoint what successful advisors have found to be the surest methods for finding the best clients.

| exhibit 8.2 | Finding the Best Clients |

**SOURCE OF THE
BEST CLIENTS**　　● CURRENT CLIENTS　　● CENTERS OF INFLUENCE　　● OTHER

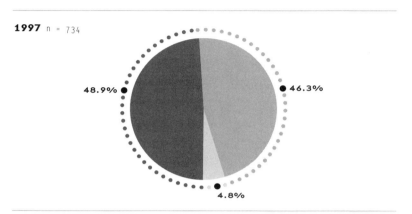

1997 n = 734

48.9%　　　46.3%

4.8%

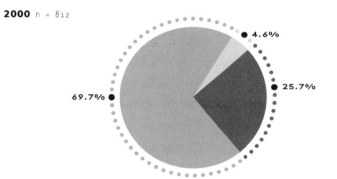

2000 n = 812

4.6%

69.7%　　25.7%

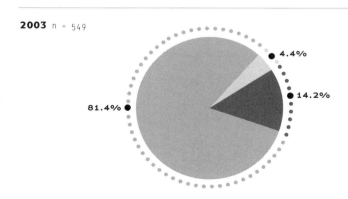

2003 n = 549

4.4%

81.4%　　14.2%

source: Prince & Associates, 1997, 2000, 2003

As you can see, over the seven-year span referrals from current clients have steadily declined while those from centers of influence have nearly doubled. One explanation, particularly from 2000 to 2003, is the general decline in investment performance. As one advisor put it, "What am I going to say to a client? 'You're down 40%, do you know anyone else who's interested in being down 40%?'" As a result, some affluent investors then turn to their other advisors, the centers of influence, for guidance, looking for a new financial advisor who's able to beat the market during a downturn or, better still, offer a wider range of wealth management choices that help cushion the blow. Further, when a client is looking for advanced planning services, the centers of influence were already the first stop, a trend that's more pronounced among the most affluent clients.

In any case, referrals are so impactful with the affluent because they want to work with experts. The services that a wealth manager provides are not tangible, and research shows that when a service is meaningful but intangible people will turn to others such as peers, business associates, or, most often, their accountants and attorneys, in order to reduce their risk of making a bad choice when selecting a wealth manager. Further, the desire on the part of the affluent to work with authorities is compounded by their inability to identify those authorities, and the best way to find out if someone is an authority is to get the opinions of other people or other experts who have worked with them and know first-hand the caliber of their work.

In addition, as we noted earlier, the wealthy want to work with advisors who have other wealthy clients. After all, who would want to have their Ferrari serviced at a Hyundai dealership?

ı comparing client referrals and referrals from centers of influence

Referrals are the best way to get new affluent clients. Moreover, with a great many investment portfolios adversely affected by the decline in the stock market since 2000, the importance of centers of influence in sourcing new clients has become ever greater. And the richer the client, the more likely they are to rely on centers of influence. By examining referrals from clients and centers of influence side-by-side, we can see the latter offer a more powerful prospecting strategy (Exhibit 8.3).

exhibit 8.3	client referrals compared to referrals from centers of influence	
FACTORS	**CLIENT REFERRALS**	**PROFESSIONAL REFERRALS**
Number of potential referrals	Relatively few	Potentially extensive
Opportunity to refer	Limited	Extensive
Extent of pre-qualification	Low to Moderate	High
Likelihood of accepting the referral	Low to Moderate	Moderate to High

Take the number of potential referrals, for example. In general, your other clients will tend to know a relatively small number of qualified wealthy clients. On the other hand, think of how many affluent clients a trusts and estates lawyer or a tax specialist has. By working with those centers of influence who themselves concentrate on the affluent market, you'll potentially be able to access a steady stream of new wealthy clients for your wealth management practice.

Further, your other wealthy clients have a limited opportunity to make a referral because such topics as estate planning or tax-efficient investing don't often come up in everyday conversation. And we all know how difficult it can be when you ask a client to provide a referral. In contrast, centers of influence are not similarly constrained. In fact, it's their job to be on the look-out for issues that their wealthy clients need resolved and for the experts whose knowledge and skills are necessary to achieve that resolution. By properly educating attorneys and accountants on the value you can bring to their clients, the door will open to many more opportunities for you to meet their clients.

When it comes to pre-qualifying wealthy prospects, the advantage again goes to the centers of influence. Clients who refer affluent clients usually only have a vague idea of their net-worth or investable assets. Accountants and attorneys, in contrast, have extensive knowledge of the finances and needs of their affluent clients.

In addition, because accountants and attorneys understand what their clients are looking for more than a friend might, there's a better chance that referrals they make will actually turn into business.

In sum, affluent client referrals are, and will remain, an important way for you to get more wealthy clients. At the same time, it's highly advisable to build strong referral networks with account-ants and attorneys.

| How women of wealth choose financial Advisors

A recent study of 743 wealthy women that we conducted in 2003 further underscored the power of centers of influence (Exhibit 8.4). To be eligible for our study, the respondents had to have $3 million or more in investable assets (the average was $6.53 million) and they had to be the principal decision-maker with respect to investment decisions involving those assets. As you can see, better than two-thirds of the respondents looked to other advisors for guidance.

exhibit 8.4	Importance of each method in finding the person who is now the primary financial advisor

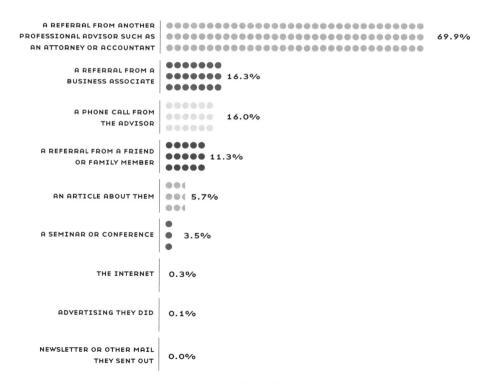

A REFERRAL FROM ANOTHER PROFESSIONAL ADVISOR SUCH AS AN ATTORNEY OR ACCOUNTANT — 69.9%

A REFERRAL FROM A BUSINESS ASSOCIATE — 16.3%

A PHONE CALL FROM THE ADVISOR — 16.0%

A REFERRAL FROM A FRIEND OR FAMILY MEMBER — 11.3%

AN ARTICLE ABOUT THEM — 5.7%

A SEMINAR OR CONFERENCE — 3.5%

THE INTERNET — 0.3%

ADVERTISING THEY DID — 0.1%

NEWSLETTER OR OTHER MAIL THEY SENT OUT — 0.0%

n = 743 women of wealth. Source: Prince & Associates, 2003.

❙ The Role of Wealth Management in Garnering Referrals

In today's financial services environment, wealth management is a made-to-order way to build a highly successful advisory practice. Because wealth managers are working to solve financial problems for affluent clients and not simply selling product, they are not pigeonholed as to what they can or can't do, and that improves their chances for getting referrals.

One of the fundamental wealth management tools, the Whole Client Model, can be very beneficial in this regard. Merely asking a client or an accountant or attorney "Do you know anyone who needs a wealth manager?" can be a hit-or-miss proposition, mostly miss. The key to success is the higher level of specificity that the Whole Client Model facilitates. So you might instead say to a client "Tell me about your friends who are business owners." If you're talking to an attorney, you might ask "How do you partner with clients who are charitably inclined?" and use information you've gathered from your own philanthropic clients as a launching point for a conversation about collaboration. By using the Whole Client Model to create a comprehensive picture of a client - by better serving your clients - you're not only identifying clients who you can be referred to but also advisors who may refer you to their clients.

❙ Creating Strategic Partnerships with Accountants and Attorneys

Up to this point, we've argued that to significantly grow a wealth management practice you'll have to refocus on your clients, transitioning some to other advisors, moving others to the wealth management model, and looking for new wealth management clients. We've also seen that the best source of new affluent clients is attorneys and accountants.

In cultivating centers of influence, most advisors enter into strategic alliances. In the context of wealth management, you would work to stay in front of the attorney or accountant; bring the center of influence leading investment ideas, tax strategies and products; and sometimes, in the case of accountants, even establish a joint-venture. However, singularly or in combination, such alliances only lead to client referrals on an intermittent and infrequent basis. To create a steady stream of new clients, you might want to consider taking the next step and establish a strategic partnership. Unlike a strategic alliance, your partner would actively make referrals to you and would make them on a regular basis.

The first step of this systematic process is to define your value proposition for affluent clients, your positioning as a wealth manager. Next, you need to articulate that value proposition for the specific centers of influence you want to form a strategic partnership with. To do so, you need to have an in-depth understanding of the particular accountant's or attorney's practice, which in turn means profiling them. Here are some of the questions you might ask to develop that profile:

- How does your work today compare to what you thought it would be when you first started out?
- What does it mean to you to "build up your practice?"
- What is the role of [your product and service] in the planning you do for your clients?
- How familiar are you with [my product and service]?
- How aware are you of the various state-of-the-art strategies that incorporate [my product and service]?
- What are the sources of revenue for your practice?
- How many wealthy clients do you have [based on your definition of affluence]?
- How do you prospect for new wealthy clients?
- How many new wealthy clients do you usually get in a year?

In profiling the attorney or accountant, you'll also learn what you'll have to do to create the strategic partnership. Nearly every accountant or attorney is open to the idea of working with a wealth manager that demonstrates integrity and technical expertise, so you must come through on both counts, establishing your integrity through referrals and interactions and establishing your professional credentials by showing the depth, breadth, and expertise of your advisory network. Finally, the relationship will depend on the financial incentives, direct or indirect, that you work out.

case study

The power of profiling

Harold, a wealth manager, was bouncing from one trusts and estates attorney to another presenting the latest and greatest tax strategy or investment management approach. He then profiled the attorneys and narrowed his list to five who had the appropriate affluent clientele, who saw the value in his wealth management platform, and with whom he felt he could connect and do business. With one of the attorneys who specialized in divorced clients, for example, Harold presented a set of complete tax and financial solutions to a complicated settlement he had overseen. As a result, Harold came away with eight new affluent clients.

ı sourcing new clients

As a wealth manager, you'll find there are going to be more ways for you to get new clients. In the meantime, you should determine where your new clients are coming from today. By understanding how you acquire new clients, you'll be better able to leverage the broader menu of wealth management, get additional clients, and extend your relationships with your current clients.

SOURCE OF NEW CLIENTS	NUMBER OF NEW CLIENTS IN THE LAST 6 TO 12 MONTHS	AVERAGE REVENUE PER NEW CLIENT	TOTAL (MULTIPLY THE 2 COLUMNS)
CURRENT CLIENTS			
ACCOUNTANT REFERRALS			
LAWYER REFERRALS			
OTHER FINANCIAL ADVISORS PROVIDING REFERRALS			
REFERRALS FROM INSIDE THE FIRM WHERE YOU WORK			
SEMINARS			
PUBLIC RELATIONS/ ADVERTISING			
DIRECT MAIL			
COLD CALLING			
OTHER			

As noted, there's no one way to get new affluent clients. In theory, cold calling can work. The question is what is the best way for you to win those clients, given such assets as your current client base, your contacts in the advisory world, and your interpersonal skills.

By looking at the above totals, you can see which prospecting approach is most profitable. Now, think in terms of being a wealth manager employing the Total Client Value algorithm. As you are now able to generate considerably more revenue per client, which prospecting approach is best?

If you're like most advisors, referrals from clients and center of influence are the optimal ways to get new affluent clients. Assuming that's the case, you should also think through how you would get referrals from:

A CURRENT CLIENT:

_____

_____

_____

AN ACCOUNTANT:

_____

_____

_____

AN ATTORNEY:

_____

_____

_____

making the grade

After each chapter in this book, we've appended a self-diagnostic exercise to help you get a better idea of your current business model, your wealth management potential, and how to best realize that potential. In this appendix, we've gathered those exercises together for your convenience and review. We've also listed the basic action steps that need to be considered before you make the commitment to wealth management.

Remember, a passing grade is a great first step but no guarantee of success; there's still plenty of hard work to be done on the way to becoming a wealth manager. But these exercises will help you understand how far you have to go and how you can get there.

action steps

DECIDE IF THE WEALTH MANAGEMENT MODEL IS RIGHT FOR YOU.

- Does wealth management make your practice better?

- Is it what your current and prospective clients need?

- Are you willing to commit yourself to wealth management?

BUILD YOUR WEALTH MANAGEMENT TEAM.

- What specialists do you need?

- Which team structure is right for you?

- What will you need to do to most effectively manage the team?

BECOME ADEPT AT THE TOOLS AND PROCESSES OF WEALTH MANAGEMENT.

- The Whole Client Model.

- The Total Client Value equation.

- Strategic scenario sessions.

GO TO WORK.

- Approach your current clients with wealth management solutions in hand.

- Generate new clients through referrals from current clients and centers of influence.

self-diagnostic

ı Assessing Your potential

using the following scale, rate how satisfied you are with each of the following business objectives:

not at all satisfied   *extremely satisfied*

< 1   2   3   4   5   6   7   8   9   10 >

ı YOUR CURRENT INCOME

ı YOUR FUTURE IN THE FINANCIAL SERVICES BUSINESS

ı YOUR ABILITY TO GET WEALTHIER CLIENTS

ı YOUR OVERALL PRODUCTION

ı YOUR CAPACITY TO LEVERAGE YOUR EXISTING
   CLIENT RELATIONSHIPS INTO MORE BUSINESS

ı YOUR ABILITY TO AVOID LOSING IMPORTANT CLIENTS

ı YOUR CAPACITY TO GENERATE SIGNIFICANT ASSET GROWTH
   IRRESPECTIVE OF THE PERFORMANCE OF THE MARKETS

TOTAL

Now add up your score. If you have a score of **35** or less, then you should consider the wealth management model (a successful wealth manager would get a score of 56 or more on this self-diagnostic).

Finally, consider how wealth management is a solution to each of these issues:

Issue	The wealth management solution
YOUR CURRENT INCOME	By creating a broad, consultative relationship, wealth management sets the stage for you to provide additional revenue-generating products and services, gather more assets, and get more referrals from both existing clients and centers of influence – the attorneys and accountants who work with the wealthy.
YOUR FUTURE IN THE FINANCIAL SERVICES BUSINESS	Our extensive research has established that most affluent clients are highly receptive to the wealth management model and that it also enhances your ability to differentiate yourself from other advisors.
YOUR ABILITY TO GET WEALTHIER CLIENTS	Based on the psychology and preferences of the affluent, the wealth management model is one of the best ways to attract and retain them as clients.
YOUR OVERALL PRODUCTION	Because of your deeper understanding of your affluent clients, you'll have more touchpoints to capitalize on and more products and services to offer.
YOUR CAPACITY TO LEVERAGE YOUR EXISTING CLIENT RELATIONSHIPS INTO MORE BUSINESS	Since you have a strong working relationship with, and an informed perspective of, your current clients, they'll be receptive to the wealth management model and what it can do for them, further solidifying the relationship while potentially increasing your profitability.
YOUR ABILITY TO AVOID LOSING IMPORTANT CLIENTS	With the consultative nature of wealth management and the broader menu of products and services that you'll be able to offer in an integrated way, you'll forge strong interpersonal bonds that can help you withstand periods of poor investment performance.
YOUR CAPACITY TO GENERATE SIGNIFICANT ASSET GROWTH IRRESPECTIVE OF THE PERFORMANCE OF THE STOCK MARKET	Many of the services and products of wealth management, such as life insurance, are not tied to the stock market or even to investing.

self-Diagnostic

▮ Reviewing Industry Trends

How would you rate the impact of each of the following industry trends on your practice today? use the following scale and also specify whether this impact has been positive or negative for your practice.

little or no impact   *considerable impact*

‹ 1   2   3   4   5   6   7   8   9   10 ›

	impact	positive	negative
▮ THE INCREASE IN THE NUMBER OF MILLIONAIRES			
▮ THE DOWNTURN IN THE STOCK MARKET			
▮ INCREASED AVAILABILITY OF INFORMATION FOR INVESTORS			
▮ THE GREATER COMPLEXITY OF YOUR CLIENTS' FINANCIAL AFFAIRS			
▮ INCREASED INVOLVEMENT BY YOUR CLIENTS IN THEIR OWN FINANCIAL AFFAIRS			
▮ THE DESIRE AMONG THE AFFLUENT FOR A CONSULTATIVE RELATIONSHIP			
TOTAL			

A wealth manager would have a score of **48** or more where each of the trends is seen as positive.

All of these trends strongly enhance the ability of wealth managers to be more successful in the following ways:

- **The increase in the number of millionaires.** The benefit of this trend is straightforward: the more wealthy people there are, the more prospective clients there are.

- **The downturn in the stock market.** When the stock market was booming, everyone was an investment genius. The bursting of the equity bubble has, more than ever, made high-net-worth investors realize that they need to turn to qualified financial advisors – and they need to be broadly diversified, a strategy that those advisors can help them execute. Furthermore, the downturn has, and will continue to, thin the ranks of financial advisors, enabling the better ones to dominate the business.

- **Increased availability of information for investors.** Information and knowledge are very different, and the affluent want financial advisors who can convert raw information into actionable insights.

- **Greater complexity of financial affairs.** The more complex the client's financial affairs, the more they need a financial advisor who can bring everything together for them. They prefer a financial advisor who can manage the many financial (and related) issues they are confronted with and then provide a variety of solutions. That financial advisor is a wealth manager.

- **Increased involvement by your clients in their own financial affairs.** Because wealth managers are drawing on a network of advisors and a broad array of products and services, they're able to offer alternative solutions that their affluent clients can compare and consider.

- **The rise of the consultative relationship among the affluent.** The wealthy want a highly interactive relationship focused on addressing their evolving financial concerns, and the wealth management model is premised on contact and connection.

self-Diagnostic

ı Appraising Business Models

use the following scale to rate how concerned you are
about each of the following:

not at all a concern   *a very significant concern*

`< 1    2    3    4    5    6    7    8    9    10 >`

ı **FINDING WEALTHY CLIENTS**

ı **GENERATING SIGNIFICANT ASSET GROWTH**

ı **COMPETITION FOR CLIENTS**

ı **INCREASED PRESSURE TO MOVE UP-MARKET AND
DROP SMALLER CLIENTS**

ı **PREVENTING THE LOSS OF WEALTHY CLIENTS**

TOTAL

A score of **25** or higher indicates that you need to take action.
Keep in mind that the move to wealth management isn't a sure-fire
cure or the only business model that can ameliorate these concerns.
However, as we've demonstrated, it's been highly effective in
helping advisors acquire wealthy clients and their investable assets.
(In Chapter 7, we'll see how to transition those clients who stand
to be less profitable for you over the long term.)

Now that you have a feel for wealth management, take a moment
and write down your top two business concerns from the above list as
seen in the context of all three dominant business models — Wealth
Manager, Product Specialist, and Investment Generalist. In addition,
detail the ways in which you think each model can help you overcome
these concerns. While you may well find that your concerns are the
same in each case, based on what we have discussed so far, the
wealth management model is best suited to address them.

wealth manager

CONCERNS   SOLUTION

1.

2.

product specialist

CONCERNS   SOLUTION

1.

2.

investment generalist

CONCERNS   SOLUTION

1.

2.

self-Diagnostic

ı understanding the critical success factors

Rate the following key attributes on a scale of 1 to 10 where 1 is for an attribute that you don't have and 10 is one that you count among your core strengths.

lacking the attribute   *core strength*

`< 1    2    3    4    5    6    7    8    9    10 >`

■ A STRONG COMMITMENT TO DOING WHAT'S BEST
FOR YOUR CLIENTS

■ A CONSULTATIVE VERSUS A "PRODUCT-PUSHING" ORIENTATION

■ THE ABILITY TO BUILD RAPPORT WITH THE WEALTHY

■ A DESIRE TO ALWAYS GET BETTER AS AN ADVISOR

■ THE ABILITY TO WORK WELL WITH OTHER PROFESSIONALS

TOTAL

We believe that every financial advisor needs to post a high score on this self-diagnostic whether they're striving to be wealth managers or not, but to compete in the wealth management arena, you should have a score of **40** or better.

This diagnostic is not about products or technical issues. It's about you and the skills you would need to deliver the wealth management model.

- **A strong commitment to doing what's best for your clients.** Aside from being the right course of action for many advisors, the very act of adopting and implementing the wealth management model helps foster this point of view. Indeed, your financial position is likely to be enhanced by it as well as by the fact that wealth management is not tied to just one or two products.

- **A consultative versus a "product-pushing" orientation.** By being consultative, you would be able to develop a deeper understanding of what your affluent clients need and want and then provide the appropriate services and products. In contrast, financial advisors with a "product" orientation have a limited audience.

- **The ability to build rapport with the wealthy.** Unless you can build rapport with the wealthy, you won't be successful. As noted, the consultative orientation of the wealth management model fosters rapport. That experience in relationship building will also help you cultivate new clients.

- **A desire to always get better as an advisor.** We feel this is paramount to success in the financial services industry, and it's particularly important with respect to the wealth management model. Take, for instance, the fact that a wealth manager must stay current with changing affluent market trends, regulatory changes, and state-of-the-art products and services. Unless, you're committed to always improving as a practitioner, you're going to be left behind in this fast-moving financial services environment.

- **The ability to work well with other professionals.** As we've said, it's impossible to deliver wealth management all by yourself; it's a team activity. That's why you should be prepared to establish solid working relationships, incorporate complementary skills and working styles, and clearly define roles and responsibilities for team members.

self-diagnostic

❙ evaluating your technical competencies

before assembling your advisory resources, it's important to get a better idea of what you do - and don't - know about the three component parts of wealth management: brokerage, investment management, and advanced planning.

on page 95, we provided a checklist of the basic wealth management products, services, and strategies. in the following exercise, we'll provide examples of how you should assess your competence for a specific element of each wealth management component. keep in mind that you can conduct similar exercises for all of the items on page 95 (and others) as they come up in your practice and then decide how much expertise you need to tap into.

using the scale below, rate how adept you are at each of the following:

not at all competent   *extremely competent*

| < | 1 | 2 | 3 | 4 | 5 | 6 | 7 | 8 | 9 | 10 | > |

❙ In considering **brokerage**, let's look at managing a concentrated stock position as an example.

❙ PURCHASE OF PUTS

❙ ZERO PREMIUM COLLARS

❙ PUT SPREAD COLLARS

❙ MONETIZED COLLARS

❙ VARIABLE PRE-PAID FORWARDS

❙ 90% NON-RECOURSE LOANS

If your score for any of the above is less than **7**, you need to learn more or bring in a specialist.

▌ Now let's focus on an element of **investment management**, portfolio construction and maintenance. For each of the following components of portfolio management, rate your competency using the same scale:

▪ PORTFOLIO CONSTRUCTION ⬜

▪ BENCHMARKING ⬜

▪ SECURITY SELECTION ⬜

▪ ASSET ALLOCATION ⬜

▪ SECTOR WEIGHTING ⬜

▪ PERFORMANCE ATTRIBUTION ⬜

▪ RISK DISPERSION ⬜

▪ PORTFOLIO POSITIONING ⬜

Again, a score of **7** or less for any discipline means you'll either need to become more expert in the area or have to outsource the function. Remember that there are a lot of top financial advisors who readily recognize their lack of expertise in these areas. Instead of doing money management themselves, for instance, they use packaged products such as mutual funds and managed accounts to provide discretionary portfolio management.

| Finally, let's examine more closely a specific area of **advanced planning**, charitable giving:

- **OUTRIGHT GIFTS**
- **CHARITABLE BEQUESTS**
- **LIFE INSURANCE**
- **GIFT ANNUITIES**
- **POOLED INCOME FUNDS**
- **CHARITABLE REMAINDER TRUSTS**
- **CHARITABLE LEAD TRUSTS**
- **DONOR-ADVISED FUNDS**
- **SUPPORTING ORGANIZATIONS**
- **PRIVATE FOUNDATIONS**

A score of less than **7** for any of the above is a signal that you must either enhance your knowledge concerning this type of charitable giving product/strategy or bring in the requisite expertise.

self-diagnostic

ı centering the Advisory Team

You and the members of your advisory team will all benefit by keeping everyone on the same page at all times. We've found the following exercise can be useful in that regard. Note: This exercise can be conducted face to face or over the phone.

ı WHAT HAVE WE BEEN TRYING TO ACCOMPLISH?

ı WHAT HAVE WE BEEN DOING THAT WORKS WELL?

ı WHAT HAVE WE BEEN DOING THAT HASN'T WORKED WELL?

ı WHAT OPPORTUNITIES ARE WE MISSING?

ı WHICH WEALTH MANAGEMENT PRODUCT OR SERVICE DO WE WANT TO USE NEXT?

ı WHAT ARE WE GOING TO DO TO MOVE THE PRACTICE FORWARD?

Think of this exercise in the way that NFL coaches might act after a game, whether the team won or lost: They would sit down and watch the game films, evaluate the performance, and get ready for the next game with the intent of doing much better.

Keep in mind that there are no right or wrong answers to these questions. They're intended to help everyone involved understand where the practice has been successful and where it may have hit a speed bump or two. The questions are also helpful when it comes to getting everyone on the team involved and looking ahead.

What have we been trying to accomplish? This gives you the opportunity to survey the members of your advisory team, to better understand their business perspectives, and to see if there's any dissension or confusion among the specialists. You can reaffirm the benefits of wealth management and reinforce how it's not only the model that affluent clients want, but it's potentially more profitable for everyone on the team. In the process, you can also redirect your collective efforts in any new direction and, most importantly, build a unified vision for the team.

What have we been doing that works well? By asking this question, you'll be able to get a clear understanding of what's working well for both the client and the specialist. It also gives you the chance to reaffirm how well the specialists have been performing and how much energy they've been expending on behalf of the team.

What have we been doing that hasn't worked well? A more complicated prospect, this will allow you to address, and hopefully fix, any glitches that may have come up along the way. For your part, it's vital not to be accusing — good or bad, what's been accomplished should be seen in the context of the team as a whole. It will also give you the chance to see how the specialists react and respond to criticism: Will they bite back or will they learn from their mistakes and try to do better next time?

What opportunities are we missing? In the course of working with clients and one another, the team members should regularly be discovering new ways to package their individual or collective services. This, after all, is one of the key premises that drives wealth management: The more you know about your clients, the more products and services you can deliver to them in a holistic way. As the partnership evolves, new ways of introducing the specialists and their services should regularly present themselves.

Which wealth management product or service do we want to use next? A follow-up to the previous question, this will help you see which specific products and services might be appropriate for individual clients based on the client/specialist interactions to date.

What are we going to do to move the practice forward? No matter how successful the team may be, there will always be the opportunity to improve. Forward progress may be a matter of entering into alliances or more formal arrangements with accountants or attorneys, or it may involve understanding and integrating the latest and greatest wealth management products and services that the team specialists may be aware of before they hit the mainstream (the latter being one of the main reasons for having the specialists on hand in the first place). In either case, forward-thinking and forward-planning will also build team spirit and solidarity.

self-diagnostic
ı grading your clients

To get an idea of the additional value and revenue that wealth management can uncover in your current client roster, use the grid below to assess the total client value of ten of your better clients. Start by identifying which services and products you're providing today as well as the revenues generated. As a wealth manager, consider what additional pools of investable assets are potentially available as well as those other services and products that you're going to provide. In addition, come up with a ballpark number for the revenues that referrals from this client could produce in a year. Then add up the numbers and rank the clients based on their total client value.

CLIENT	CURRENT AUM	ADDITIONAL INVESTABLE ASSETS	ADDITIONAL SERVICES- PRODUCTS	REFERRALS (QUANTIFIED)	TOTAL

CURRENT REVENUE $ _____

TOTAL POTENTIAL REVENUES AS A WEALTH MANAGER $ _____

self-diagnostic

ı sourcing new clients

As a wealth manager, you'll find there are going to be more ways for you to get new clients. In the meantime, you should determine where your new clients are coming from today. By understanding how you acquire new clients, you'll be better able to leverage the broader menu of wealth management, get additional clients, and extend your relationships with your current clients.

SOURCE OF NEW CLIENTS	NUMBER OF NEW CLIENTS IN THE LAST 6 TO 12 MONTHS	AVERAGE REVENUE PER NEW CLIENT	TOTAL (MULTIPLY THE 2 COLUMNS)
CURRENT CLIENTS			
ACCOUNTANT REFERRALS			
LAWYER REFERRALS			
OTHER FINANCIAL ADVISORS PROVIDING REFERRALS			
REFERRALS FROM INSIDE THE FIRM WHERE YOU WORK			
SEMINARS			
PUBLIC RELATIONS/ ADVERTISING			
DIRECT MAIL			
COLD CALLING			
OTHER			

As noted, there's no one way to get new affluent clients. In theory, cold calling can work. The question is what is the best way for you to win those clients, given such assets as your current client base, your contacts in the advisory world, and your interpersonal skills.

By looking at the above totals, you can see which prospecting approach is most profitable. Now, think in terms of being a wealth manager employing the Total Client Value algorithm. As you are now able to generate considerably more revenue per client, which prospecting approach is best?

If you're like most advisors, referrals from clients and center of influence are the optimal ways to get new affluent clients. Assuming that's the case, you should also think through how you would get referrals from:

A CURRENT CLIENT:

_____

_____

_____

AN ACCOUNTANT:

_____

_____

_____

AN ATTORNEY:

_____

_____

_____

about the authors

HANNAH SHAW GROVE

Ms. Grove is an executive with a leading Wall Street firm and has more than 15 years of financial services experience. She is an authority on investments and related solutions for institutional and high-net-worth investors, and works regularly with wealth managers on sophisticated planning and servicing techniques. She is a noted columnist and speaker and a cum laude graduate of Harvard University.

RUSS ALAN PRINCE
www.iihighnetworth.com

Mr. Prince, president of the market research and consulting firm Prince & Associates Inc., is a leading expert on the private wealth industry and on advisor-based distribution.

Mr. Prince consults for leading financial institutions on strategic and marketing issues and provides a variety of coaching and consulting services to professional advisors who focus on affluent markets. He is a seasoned developer of proprietary prospecting and sales and relationship management systems, and also provides high-end customized practice management and marketing programs.